The Beatles

LEADING THE BRITISH INVASION

By Diane Dakers

Crabtree Publishing Company

www.crabtreebooks.com

Crabtree Publishing Company

www.crabtreebooks.com

Author: Diane Dakers
Publishing plan research and development:
  Sean Charlebois, Reagan Miller
  Crabtree Publishing Company
Project coordinator: Mark Sachner,
  Water Buffalo Books
Editors: Mark Sachner, Lynn Peppas
Proofreader: Wendy Scavuzzo
Indexer: Gini Holland
Editorial director: Kathy Middleton
Photo researcher: Ruth Owen
Designer: Alix Wood
Production coordinator: Margaret Amy Salter
Production: Kim Richardson
Prepress technician: Margaret Amy Salter
Print coordinator: Katharine Berti

Written, developed, and produced by
Water Buffalo Books

Photographs and reproductions:
Alamy: Keystone Pictures USA: p. 20, 22, 37; Pictorial Press: p. 29, 82;
  A.F. Archive: p. 48; Trinity Mirror/Mirrorpix: p. 49, 51, 58, 84
Associated Press: cover (bottom right); PA Wire URN:13708066
  (Press Association via AP Images): cover (bottom left)
Corbis: Michael Ochs Archives: p. 9; Bettmann: p. 67, 73
Dreamstime: p. 64; Paul Mckinnon: p. 96
Getty Images: Mark and Colleen Hayward: p.12; Keystone: p. 15 (top), 17;
  Michael Ochs Archives: p. 34, 71; Express: p. 89; Terry O'Neill: p. 90
Mark J. Sachner: p. 1, 46 (top), 54, 66, 80, 81, 94, 95
Public Domain: p. 5, 11, 15 (bottom left), 15
  (bottom right), 24 (top right), 24 (bottom left), 26, 31, 50 (right),
  53, 57 (left), 59 (top), 59 (bottom left), 59 (bottom right), 62, 63 (top),
  63 (bottom), 73, 79, 93 (top), 98, 103
Rex Features: Nils Jorgensen: p. 68
Shutterstock: cover (top), Neftali: p. 4, 87; Jomar Aplaon: p. 7, 40;
  Bruce Yeung: p. 24 (top left); Helga Esteb: p. 24 (center); Nito:
  p. 32 (left), 57 (right); Dario Sabljak: p. 32 (right); Scott Kapich:
  p. 46 (bottom); Andy Lidstone: p. 65, 69, 77, 91, 93; Lisa Fischer:
  p. 76; StampGirl: p. 87; Jaguar PS: p. 97; Mazzzur: p. 9 (bottom);
  Joe Seer: p. 100 (top center); S. Bukley: p. 100 (top right); Featureflash:
  p. 100 (bottom left), 100 (bottom center)
Wikipedia Creative Commons: Heinrich Klaffs: p. 24 (bottom right);
  Raymond Arritt: p. 38; Jean Fortunet: p. 99 (top); Susan Beals:
  p. 100 (top left); Kubacheck: p. 100 (bottom right); Timmo Warner:
  p. 101; p. 42, 45, 50 (left), 61, 86

Publisher's note:
All quotations in this book come from original sources and contain the spelling and grammatical inconsistencies of the original text. Some of the quotations may also contain terms that are no longer in use and may be considered inappropriate or offensive. The use of such terms is for the sake of preserving the historical and literary accuracy of the sources and should not be seen as encouraging or endorsing the use of such terms today.

Cover: The Beatles were a band from Liverpool, England, who went on to become a music phenomenon around the world. Musical and cultural trendsetters, their career spanned the entire decade of the colorful and tumultuous 1960s. Even though they stopped touring as a band in 1966, these pop-song mop tops grew to become mature and influential artists whose songs are still considered standards today. Historians, journalists, and scholars have studied the Beatles from every possible angle, trying to unlock the secret to their never-ending appeal.

Library and Archives Canada Cataloguing in Publication

Dakers, Diane
       The Beatles : leading the British invasion / Diane Dakers.

(Crabtree groundbreaker biographies)
Includes index.
Issued also in electronic formats.
ISBN 978-0-7787-1035-6 (bound).--ISBN 978-0-7787-1045-5 (pbk.)

       1. Beatles--Juvenile literature. 2. Rock musicians--England--Biography--Juvenile literature. I. Title. II. Series: Crabtree groundbreaker biographies

  ML3930.B39D135 2013   j782.42166092'2   C2012-908513-8

Library of Congress Cataloging-in-Publication Data

Dakers, Diane.
       The Beatles : leading the British invasion / Diane Dakers.
       pages cm. -- (Crabtree groundbreaker biographies)
Includes index.
 ISBN 978-0-7787-1035-6 (reinforced library binding : alk. paper) --
ISBN 978-0-7787-1045-5 (pbk. : alk. paper) -- ISBN 978-1-4271-9247-9
(electronic pdf) -- ISBN 978-1-4271-9171-7 (electronic html)
 1. Beatles--Juvenile literature. 2. Rock musicians--England--Biography--
Juvenile literature. I. Title.

 ML3930.B35D35 2013
 782.42166092'2--dc23
 [B]

                                                          2012049884

Crabtree Publishing Company

www.crabtreebooks.com   1-800-387-7650

Printed in Canada/052014/TT20140331

Published
in Canada
Crabtree Publishing
616 Welland Ave.
St. Catharines, Ontario
L2M 5V6

Published in
the United States
Crabtree Publishing
PMB 59051
350 Fifth Ave., 59th Floor
New York, NY 10118

Published in the
United Kingdom
Crabtree Publishing
Maritime House
Basin Road North, Hove
BN41 1WR

Published
in Australia
Crabtree Publishing
3 Charles Street
Coburg North
VIC, 3058

Contents

Chapter 1
"To the Toppermost"

On December 10, 1963, CBS aired a British interview with a group of musicians who were insanely popular in their native country and were about to become a sensation on the other side of the Atlantic as well. The group was the Beatles, and the CBS story was a first for them—an interview, plus a music clip, shown in the United States. Watching the news that night was 15-year-old Marsha Albert, who lived in a suburb of Washington, D.C. She liked what she heard, and she wrote a letter to her local disc jockey, or DJ, Carroll James of WWDC radio, telling him so. She also urged him to start playing Beatles music on the air. James had seen the same story, and he arranged for a Beatles record to be hand-carried from Britain to the United States by a flight attendant. The name of the record: "I Want to Hold Your Hand."

The Fab Four
The record was one that Capitol hadn't planned to release until January 1964. When Carroll played it on his show, though, the switchboard at WWDC lit up like a Christmas tree. The response was so huge that Capitol moved its national release date up to December 26. Beatlemania was under way in America!

Opposite: The Beatles have long been the subject of instant recognition all over the world. Around 2001, the Central Asian nation of Kyrgystan issued this set of postage stamps honoring the Fab Four and depicting their "look" at various times during their history as a band.

5

CATCH IT ON YOUR SCREEN!

Catch Beatlemania, witness the British Invasion, and look in on any of the other recording artists discussed in this book—including members of the Beatles when they went solo and recorded songs on their own—by going online. Just visit www.youtube.com and key in the names of the performers or their songs. See what it was like to watch the Beatles for the first time on *The Ed Sullivan Show* or hear "I Want to Hold Your Hand" the way North American kids did back in 1964!

By the time the Beatles arrived in the United States two months later, "I Want to Hold Your Hand" had already shot to #1 on the record charts, and celebrity host Ed Sullivan had already booked them for three appearances on his top-rated TV variety show. In addition, concert promoters were scrambling to book the band into U.S. stadiums and arenas.

What made the Beatles' popularity even more surprising was the fact that the "Fab Four," as they quickly came to be called—John Lennon, Paul McCartney, George Harrison, and Ringo Starr—were barely out of their teens, and they had been together as the Beatles for less than three years. Nobody, especially the boys themselves, could have predicted the welcome they would receive from American fans. In fact, on the plane from London to New York, they were worried that nobody would be at the airport to greet them! As it was, thousands of screaming fans and dozens of reporters and photographers showed up to welcome them.

From their legendary appearances on *The Ed Sullivan Show* in February 1964, through to their final concert in San Francisco in 1966, the Beatles owned the American music scene. They had already taken over the record charts and concert world in Britain, and they would soon conquer all of Europe, Asia, and Australia.

The British Invasion Is Launched

The Beatles' music was groundbreaking in its day. Until then, American songwriters and musicians had dominated the pop culture world. The Beatles brought a new sound—a distinctly British sound—that paved the way for what became known as the British Invasion.

BEATLES IN CANADA

The Beatles actually "arrived" in Canada a long time before they were known south of the border because Capitol Records-Canada negotiated its record deals separately from Capitol Records-U.S. The Beatles' first single, "Love Me Do," was released in Canada in February 1963—four months after its debut in Britain—and more than a year before its U.S. release.

"I used to listen to about 50 new records a week," said Capitol Canada executive Paul White. "Then one day I put on 'Love Me Do' by a group called the Beatles. I immediately sat up and took notice. The sound was so different, so completely fresh. I'm certainly not going to claim that I could read the future, and already knew how big the Beatles were going to be, but I did like them a lot, and wanted Capitol of Canada to get in on the ground floor. I decided to release Beatles' records in Canada."

The Fab Four's first North American album *Beatlemania! With the Beatles* was also released by Capitol Canada in November 1963, two months before the first U.S. album. By the spring of 1964, Capitol Canada and Capitol U.S. had each released three Beatles albums. After that, the two Capitols got together and released subsequent albums jointly.

RECORDS, SINGLES, LPS

Before there were CDs and iTunes, and even before there were cassette tapes, there were records. The vinyl discs have become popular again with nightclub DJs, but in the days of the Beatles, records were the only way to buy music. If you liked a particular song, you could buy it as a single— a small record with one song on the A side and another, usually less popular, song on the B side. An LP (which stands for "long-playing") was a record featuring a collection of tunes.

Early recordings of Beatles' singles.

At first, Beatles tunes were young, peppy, and fun, just like the Fab Four themselves. The "lads" were cute, charming, and sincere. They dressed in an unusual style and wore their hair long. They were funny. They could laugh at themselves and banter with reporters, unlike other more serious and sullen rock stars of the day.

In later years, the Beatles' music became more inventive and thoughtful. The lads from Liverpool, England, grew up in front of the world and spoke their minds through their music. Their lyrics rang true for young people unhappy with the state of their world. They embodied the musical, artistic, social, and spiritual promise of an entire generation. "The boys served as hip role models for a restless generation of Americans grappling with questions of individual freedom and expression," wrote biographer Bob Spitz.

In the recording studio, the Beatles' cutting-edge technologies were so elaborate that the resulting songs couldn't be repeated in performance. Despite the absence of touring as a way to promote record sales, the foursome recorded more music than ever. For 10 years, this band cranked out records at an astonishing pace, each album outselling the last.

Growing Apart, Together Forever

Over time, though, egos and artistic differences drove the group apart. As one historian wrote on the website www.beatles-history.net: "The brotherhood of these four men had dissipated... They had grown up together, and had grown creatively together, but with all the talent between them, they were eager to each pursue their own interests. They each wanted total control of their creative endeavors, and they each went off in slightly different directions."

After the Beatles broke up in 1970, they became four solo artists who took their private animosity public before eventually settling into cordial post-Beatles relationships. Sadly, John Lennon was murdered before he had fully reconciled his differences with Paul and George.

Even though the Beatles have neither performed nor recorded as a group for more than 50 years, they remain the top-selling band of all time. Since they split up, more than 40 Beatles compilation, or collection, albums have been released and continue to sell by the millions. In the year after John's 1980 murder alone, 75 million Beatles records were sold worldwide.

Dozens of books, hundreds of academic papers, and thousands of blogs and websites are dedicated to the Fab Four today. Despite being the Beatles for less than a decade, John, Paul, George and Ringo together formed the most successful—and arguably the most influential—musical group in history.

As boys growing up in working-class England, though, they were like hundreds of other lads who dreamed of becoming rich and famous rock stars. Little did they know how quickly their dreams would come true.

John Lennon, Ringo Starr, Paul McCartney, and George Harrison work their charm on reporters—and a somewhat amused-looking security guard—at a press conference during their U.S. trip in February 1964.

Chapter 2
Four Fab Individuals

Before they became known around the world as "The Fab Four," John, Paul, George and Ringo were just four kids from Liverpool. They grew up in the same schools and neighborhoods, near a street named Penny Lane and an orphanage called Strawberry Field. Each of the lads discovered his passion for music individually, but it was that shared passion that eventually drew them together to become the Beatles.

Introducing John Lennon

John Lennon was born on October 9, 1940, during World War II. At the time, his hometown was in the middle of what was called the "Liverpool Blitz," a 10-month period of continual German air raids.

FOR THE RECORD...

Many biographies say that when John Lennon was born, bombs were shattering the city all around him. In 2006, a researcher put that myth to rest. There are no newspaper, military, or German records of an air raid over Liverpool on October 9, 1940. The following day, however, October 10, was a day of significant bombing—and baby John was still in the hospital at that time. Some biographers have said the newborn spent many hours under a hospital bed to protect him from flying debris. This is probably true, but not on the day he was born.

John's father, Alfred, better known as "Alf" or "Freddie," was a merchant sailor who worked as a steward and a waiter on ocean-going ships. He was away at sea the day his son was born—and for the first five years of the boy's life. John's mother, Julia, had worked at a movie theater until she married Alf in 1938.

John is shown with his mother Julia in 1949, at around the age of nine.

Both sides of the family had musical roots. Alf's Irish father, whose last name was originally O'Leannain, sang with a musical group in the United States. Julia's grandfather (John's great-grandfather) had also been a professional musician. While Julia and Alf were not professional musicians, they loved to sing, and they each played banjo.

When John was four, his mother, tired of being alone while her husband was at sea, had an affair with a Welsh soldier stationed nearby. He left her when she became pregnant. Julia never saw the man again but, in June 1945, she gave birth to his daughter, John's half-sister, Victoria Elizabeth. Unable to raise two children on her own, Julia gave the baby up for adoption.

In 1946, Alf returned to Liverpool to resume his life with Julia and John. By then, Julia was living with the man who would be, for the rest of her life, her common-law partner (that is, her partner by informal agreement, rather than by law). When Julia rejected Alf's offer to return

JOHN'S LONG-LOST SIBLING

In 1966, Ingrid Maria Pederson, a nurse in Norway, was about to get married and she needed to find her birth certificate. She located the document in her mother's closet and was shocked by what it said. "I found a yellowing, dog-eared adoption paper that had been issued by Liverpool County Court," she said years later. "Then I saw my full name: Lillian Ingrid Maria Pedersen, and my birth date. Above that were the three words I had been looking for: Victoria Elizabeth Lennon—the name I was born with. My real mother's name, Julia Lennon [who had given up young Victoria for adoption], was also there. I burst into tears."

Out of respect to her adoptive parents, Ingrid never told them what she had discovered. "It would have been a betrayal of them," she said. Through the height of Beatlemania, and the death of her world-famous half-brother, John Lennon, Ingrid never shared her secret. Finally, a few weeks after her mother died in 1998, she came forward to tell the world her story.

to their life together, he tried to sneak away to New Zealand with young John. Julia caught up with them before they left the country, however. Alf forced five-year-old John to choose between his parents. John said he wanted to stay with his father but, as soon as his mom started to walk away, the lad began crying and followed her. It would be 20 years before John saw his father again. He never developed a close relationship with Alf.

Julia's sister Mimi did not think Julia gave John a stable home life. She suggested the boy move in with her and her husband George, but Julia rejected the idea. Mimi returned to her sister's home with a social worker. Together, they convinced Julia the boy would be better off with his aunt and uncle. John spent the rest of his childhood living with his Aunt Mimi and Uncle George Smith, a dairy farmer.

DID YOU KNOW?

John Lennon's mother chose Winston as her son's middle name, to honor Britain's then-prime minister, Winston Churchill.

As a child, John loved books more than he loved toys. Every evening, he and Uncle George sat together and studied newspaper headlines, learning new words. By the time John started school, he could already read. John also loved to draw, and he taught himself to play the harmonica.

John, the Young Rebel

While John was still in primary school (elementary school), his rebellious streak—likely the result of his childhood turmoil—started to show itself. The school's headmaster (principal) once said that John was "as sharp as a needle, but he won't do anything he doesn't want to do."

After he graduated to Quarry Bank High School, John spent more time causing trouble, writing sassy poems, and drawing nasty pictures of his teachers, than he did on his schoolwork. In 1955, after his kindly Uncle George died suddenly, John's behavior became even worse. He skipped classes, smoked, and stole from other students. He dressed in sloppy clothes, cursed, and fought with teachers and classmates.

On the other hand, John also started spending more time with his mother during this period. She taught him to play the banjo, and the two sang together for hours. At the same time, John discovered rock 'n' roll music and American singer Elvis Presley. He identified with movies such as *Rebel Without a Cause*, starring James Dean as a leather-clad, troubled teen; and *The Wild One*, with Marlon Brando playing a motorcycle gangster—films that celebrated the defiance and scorn John felt for the world.

When he was 15, John sent away for a cheap mail-order guitar. He played it from the time he got home from school until he went to bed at night. Before long, he and his friends at Quarry Bank High School formed a skiffle band—a popular musical craze at the time. The band was called the Black Jacks, because the boys wore tight black jeans and plain white shirts. Before they ever performed in public, the musicians changed the band's name to the Quarrymen, in honor of their high school. At first, the Quarrymen played at parties, school events, and talent contests, mostly for free, just for the love of music.

As a teenager, John (shown in photo at left between George and Paul around 1960) was drawn to the rebellious looks and attitudes displayed in movies of the 1950s. Two actors whose characters influenced John included James Dean (lower left), and Marlon Brando (shown lower right in his role as motorcycle-gang leader Johnny Strabler).

Within a year, though, the band became a little more successful, playing skiffle at clubs and community events. On July 6, 1957, the Quarrymen played at a garden party at the neighborhood church, St. Peter's. After the performance, one of John's friends introduced him to another neighborhood kid—a 15-year-old named Paul.

Introducing Paul McCartney

James Paul McCartney was born June 18, 1942, during World War II. His mother Mary was a nurse and midwife, and his father Jim was a wartime volunteer firefighter. Jim was on duty

A MUSICAL CRAZE CALLED SKIFFLE

Popular during the late 1940s and early 1950s, skiffle was a mix of jazz, blues, American folk songs, and Southern spirituals. It was something that was easy to play—by almost anyone—because it didn't require expensive instruments or a lot of musical training. A typical skiffle band consisted of a cheap guitar or two, a banjo, something to drum on, and a few homemade instruments. Usually, one band member played a washboard, a corrugated metal or glass surface that was used to scrub clothing before the washing machine was invented. The performer would put sewing thimbles on his or her fingers and strum the washboard to make a rhythmic sound. Another common skiffle instrument was the "washtub," or "tea-chest" bass, made by attaching a rope to a broomstick and fastening it to an upside-down washtub or wooden crate.

Originally, skiffle bands entertained audiences at clubs between headline bands—almost anyone could jump onstage and play whatever was at hand. Eventually, skiffle became a headline musical style on its own. It was fun, it was lively, and it had a good beat. In the late 1940s, when John, Paul, George, and Ringo were developing their love of music, most of the 300-plus nightclubs in Liverpool specialized in skiffle.

when Paul, his eldest son, was born. Two years later, his son Mike was born. Before and after the war, Jim sold cotton to local stores. When he wasn't at work, he played trumpet and piano in a variety of

In this 1948 photo, Paul is shown at around six years of age, with his little brother Mike.

Liverpool jazz bands, at one point leading his own group called Jim Mac's Jazz Band. He passed his love of music on to his sons Paul and Mike.

When they were little, the boys lied down on the floor while their father played the family's piano. Jim encouraged his sons to play piano, too. "To us kids, he was a pretty good player," said Paul in a 2010 interview. "I was very influenced by him."

At school, Paul excelled. He was a hard-working, well-behaved student. At the age of 11, he was one of just four in his class to gain admission into the prestigious Liverpool Institute for Boys. At the "Inny," as the school was known, Paul proved himself a natural leader and a popular boy who excelled in art and English literature. He loved the plays of William Shakespeare, Oscar Wilde, and Tennessee Williams; the works of Welsh poet Dylan Thomas; and American novelist John Steinbeck. At the end of his third year, though, Paul discovered rock 'n' roll and became far more interested in music than in his studies.

DID YOU KNOW?

Paul McCartney still has the upright piano his father played when Paul was a boy.

For his 14th birthday, Paul's dad gave the teen a trumpet. But Paul longed for a guitar, so he could sing while he played rock 'n' roll tunes. He was hooked on Elvis Presley, Fats Domino, Buddy Holly, and other American stars. He wanted to play their kind of music. Eventually, Jim allowed his son to trade in the trumpet. "The minute he got the guitar, that was the end," said Paul's brother Mike. "He was lost. He didn't have time to eat or think about anything else."

Paul's focus on his guitar intensified a few months later when tragedy struck his family. On October 31, 1956, his mom Mary died unexpectedly of breast cancer. Paul turned to music to help him through his grief, losing himself in guitar playing and songwriting. One of the first songs Paul wrote after his mother died was called "I Lost My Little Girl."

When Paul Met John

During this time, Paul's school chum Ivan Vaughan suggested he come to the St. Peter's Church garden party to hear the Quarrymen— a band led by Ivan's friend, John Lennon. After the band's afternoon performance, Ivan introduced John to Paul, who picked up a guitar and gave the other musicians a little

PAUL'S PUBLIC DEBUT

Paul McCartney's first-ever solo public performances took place at a summer resort in Yorkshire, England. Fourteen-year-old Paul played Little Richard's "Long Tall Sally" in a talent show. At that moment, he realized he loved being onstage at the center of an audience's attention.

ON THE OTHER HAND...

Standard guitars are made for right-handed musicians. Paul McCartney is a lefty. When he got his first guitar, he struggled to play it, but he couldn't quite get the hang of it. One day, he saw a poster showing another musician playing the guitar backward—with his left hand. Paul realized that would work for him, too. He flipped his guitar over, reversed the order of the strings, and started playing brilliantly.

demonstration of his talent. "It was uncanny," said Eric Griffiths, who played guitar with the Quarrymen. "He could play and sing in a way that none of us could, including John. It was so natural."

John was taken with Paul's confidence and musical expertise—he even knew how to tune a guitar! At the same time, Paul was drawn to the rebel in John and his natural leadership and wit. A week later, having been so impressed with the 15-year-old left-handed guitarist, John Lennon and his band mates asked Paul to join the Quarrymen. He appeared with them onstage for the first time on October 18, 1957.

After Paul accepted the invitation to join the Quarrymen, he and John became close friends and musical collaborators, meeting almost every day to practice and write songs together. To John, the words were most important—his gloomy lyrics were poetic, but often contained messages too complicated for anyone else to understand. Paul, on the other hand, created straightforward, upbeat tunes that showcased his superior musical talents. The teens' opposite natures made for balanced songwriting—and a creative rivalry that pushed each of them

When this photo was taken sometime around 1960, Paul (left) and John were still sporting the 1950s British "rocker" look and they clearly enjoyed performing together. Even then, their friendship was well on its way to becoming one of the most successful songwriting partnerships in history.

to write more, and be better musicians while trying to outdo each other.

The boys didn't have a tape recorder, so they wrote down some of their lyrics and music—but they figured if they couldn't remember a song the next day, it wasn't worth remembering.

Because Paul played guitar left-handed, and John played with his right hand, they could sit across from each other, as if looking in a mirror. In this way, Paul taught John new chords and

"They were tuned to the same groove. Still, their personalities were different. Where John was impatient and careless, Paul was a perfectionist. Where John was moody and aloof, Paul was outgoing and cheerful. Where John was struggling to become a musician, Paul seemed born to it."

Beatles biographer Bob Spitz

fingering skills. "Paul taught me how to play the guitar proper," said John years later.

In the fall of 1957, while Paul was still a student at the Inny, John started studying at the Liverpool College of Art, right around the corner. As usual, he rebelled against the structure of the school, and he didn't care for the other students—except for a hip but kind and serious classmate named Stu Sutcliffe. Before long, John and Stu were best friends.

Meanwhile, at the Inny, Paul had befriended a younger boy named George, considered the best guitar player at the Liverpool Institute.

Introducing George Harrison

George Harold Harrison was born on February 25, 1943, the youngest of four children. His mother Louise was a homemaker and his father Harold was a bus driver. By the age of three, George's independent streak was already obvious. The little boy ran errands for his mom to the local grocery store. Even without a list, he never forgot anything she needed.

When he was five, George started school at Dovedale Primary, where eight-year-old John Lennon was already a student. George excelled in his classes, not because he was particularly dedicated to his studies, but because he was so intelligent that he didn't have to work hard. Good grades came naturally. He graduated easily and was accepted at the Liverpool Institute for Boys—the school Paul McCartney also attended. Paul was a year ahead of George.

For the first two years at the Inny, George pleased his parents by being a model student. He attended all his classes, paid attention to

George Harrison is shown playing the guitar as a young teen. During and following his career playing lead guitar with the Beatles, George was regarded as one of the most talented guitarists of all time.

his teachers, and studied at home in the evenings. By the time he entered his third year, though, he had discovered rock 'n' roll music and he lost interest in everything else.

At 13, George could no longer hide his distaste for the formal education system—and the people who ran it. He grew bored and refused to follow school rules or conform to a dress code. Instead of the acceptable black blazer, flannel trousers, and tie, George showed up at school in flashy, colorful clothes. He grew his hair long and slicked it back. He began smoking, skipping classes, and spending the afternoons at a local movie theater with his friend.

When he did attend classes, he didn't pay attention—instead, he sketched pictures of guitars all over his notebooks. When he heard that another student had a guitar for sale, he borrowed money from his mom to buy it. Like Paul, he threw himself into music and taught himself to play. Unlike Paul, though, George wasn't a natural musician. He worked hard to master the instrument, practicing constantly, listening to the "riffs," or musical phrases, of famous guitarists and imitating their styles. He started a skiffle band called the Rebels that ended up playing only one performance.

By that time, George had already met Paul. The two rode the same bus, which was driven by George's father, to and from school every day. It was an hour-long trip each way. The lads shared a passion for rock 'n' roll, especially guitar music. Eventually, they started practicing together in the afternoons.

ELVIS IN THE HOUSE

One day, as young George was out riding his bicycle around his neighborhood, he heard Elvis Presley's "Heartbreak Hotel" wafting through a window of a nearby house. He had never heard anything like it before. He later said he had "an epiphany," or a moment of sudden insight, then and there. From that day on, rock 'n' roll became his sole focus in life.

Early in 1958, Paul invited George to a Quarrymen performance at a local club. George brought along his guitar and, after Paul introduced him to the other members of the band, the 15-year-old gave them a taste of his talent. While the other Quarrymen were impressed by George's abilities and would have welcomed him into the band, 17-year-old John wanted nothing to do with the kid. "George was just too young," he said. "He looked even younger than Paul, and Paul looked about 10, with his baby face."

Paul was determined to have George in the band, though, so he arranged an "accidental" meeting with John on a double-decker bus. As Paul tells the story:

"George slipped quietly into one of the seats aboard this largely deserted bus we were riding, took out his guitar and went right into 'Raunchy' [a popular but difficult song of the day]. A few days later, I said to John, 'Well, what do you think?' And he finally says, 'Yeah, man, he'd be great.' And that was simply that. George was in."

UNDER THE INFLUENCE

The Beatles may have been one of the most influential bands of all times but, when they first started, other groundbreaking musicians influenced them. Pioneers of rock 'n' roll—including rhythm-and-blues (R&B) singer-songwriter Fats Domino; legendary singer/guitar player Chuck Berry; the flamboyant Little Richard; and the clean-cut Buddy Holly, who died at age 23—all inspired John, Paul, George, and Ringo. But it was Elvis Presley who really excited them. "Nothing really affected me before Elvis," John said. Paul called Elvis "the guru we'd been waiting for." Both young musicians imitated "the King," as Elvis came to be called. John began to dress, swagger, and slick back his hair like Elvis, while Paul imitated his vocal style. For George, Elvis's music "had an incredible impact on me, just because I'd never heard anything like it."

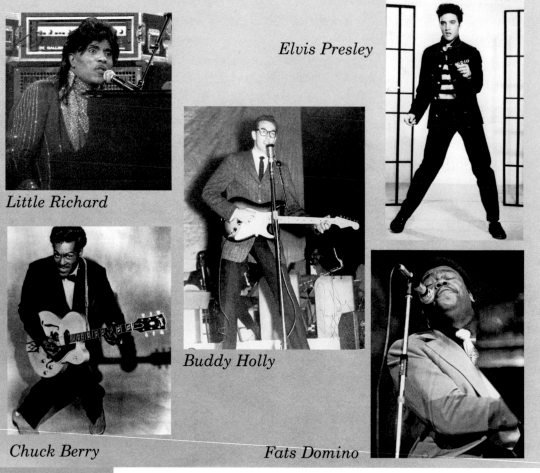

Little Richard

Elvis Presley

Buddy Holly

Chuck Berry

Fats Domino

At first, George was allowed to rehearse with the band, filling in when others were absent. But his talent far surpassed that of one of the Quarrymen's original guitarists, Eric Griffiths. John and Paul asked Eric to play electric bass instead, but Eric couldn't afford to buy one. Before long, Eric was out of the band and George was a full-time Quarryman.

Introducing Ringo Starr

The oldest Beatle, Ringo Starr, was born Richard Starkey on July 7, 1940. The only child of parents Richard and Elsie, who had met while working at a bakery, the boy was nicknamed "Ritchie." The family lived in one of the poorest parts of Liverpool, and things got even tougher for mother and son when the boy's father abandoned them when Ritchie was three. To make ends meet, Elsie started working as a server in a pub—a job she loved. Ritchie's extended family included grandparents and neighbors, who helped Elsie care for her son.

Ritchie started school at age five, but had to quit—for the first time—two years later. Just before he turned seven, Ritchie felt sharp stomach pains that turned out to be appendicitis—a dangerous swelling of the appendix. He had emergency surgery, then developed an infection that left him in a coma for 10 weeks. Doctors told Elsie to prepare herself for the worst. Her son would probably not survive his illness. Ritchie surprised them, though. He woke from the coma, only to tumble out of his hospital bed six months later. His injuries from the fall meant he had to stay in the hospital another six months!

GEORGE FAILS TO MAKE THE GRADE

As George Harrison's guitar talents increased, his grades at school fell, until he found himself at the bottom of his class. A year after he joined the Quarrymen, he left the Liverpool Institute at age 16, without graduating. He worked briefly as an apprentice electrician at a department store, until the Beatles left Liverpool for a series of performances in Germany.

Across the Airwaves

In the 1950s, American rock 'n' roll music wasn't easy to come by on British radio stations. Teenagers of the day, though, discovered that, late at night, depending on the weather, if they fiddled with the radio dial just right, they could tune into Radio Luxembourg. Broadcast from a tiny principality, or royalty-ruled state, in Europe about 600 miles (965 kilometers) southeast of Liverpool, the radio station played English-language programs that showcased popular music from the United States. Between 1954 and 1963, the station, which only broadcast in the evenings, catered to the musical tastes of teens. Three teenagers who were hooked on Radio Luxembourg were John Lennon, Paul McCartney, and George Harrison. It's where each of them first heard the big-name musicians that became so influential to them.

Bill Haley and His Comets were one of the groups that John, Paul, and George eagerly listened to on Radio Luxembourg in the 1950s. Shown here: Bill Haley (right front) and members of the Comets around 1955, shortly after the release of two of their best-known hits, "Shake, Rattle and Roll" and "Rock Around the Clock."

By the time Ritchie returned to school, he was good-natured, but far behind his classmates. He could not read or write, so his mom asked a neighbor girl to tutor him. Still, Ritchie struggled and never enjoyed school. He started playing hooky, or skipping school, which didn't help his academic performance. Just before he turned 13, another illness struck. This time, it was a lung disease called pleurisy—and this time, Ritchie stayed in the hospital for two years. During that time, he and other young patients joined the hospital band. Ritchie played "drums," banging cotton-covered sticks on a cabinet.

Ritchie never returned to school and, when he left the hospital at age 15, he found it hard to find a job. His childhood illnesses had left him too small and weak for most physical labor, and his lack of education left him few other options. He worked briefly as a messenger, but had to quit after he failed a required medical exam. Later, he was fired from his job as a bartender when he showed up for work drunk. Eventually, at 17, he landed an apprenticeship at an engineering firm.

Ritchie Discovers Drumming

By this time, Ritchie's mother Elsie had remarried painter Harry Graves. For Christmas in 1957, Harry gave Ritchie his first set of drums—a second-hand kit. "He used to practice in the back room—but only for half an hour a night," said his mother a few years later. "That was all he was allowed because of the noise!"

When a group of employees at his workplace started a skiffle band, Ritchie joined as drummer. The little group entertained co-workers on their lunch breaks and performed at parties, weddings, and other small events after hours.

Eventually, Ritchie borrowed money from his grandfather to buy a better drum set. With that, he started playing with a string of local bands, filling in wherever a drummer was needed. While playing with his workmates at a talent show one night, he met singer Alan Caldwell, who fronted his own band called Alan Caldwell and the Texans. The band needed a drummer so, starting in March 1959, Ritchie sat in with them now and again. Over the next six months, Caldwell changed his name—and the band's name—three times. He finally settled on Rory Storm and the Hurricanes. In November, Ritchie officially joined the group. "When we told him we were going to play rock 'n' roll full tilt, he said he was interested," said Johnny Byrne, the band's guitar player.

Very quickly, Rory Storm and the Hurricanes became the number one band in Liverpool and started getting bookings elsewhere in the UK. In the summer of 1960, Ritchie had a tough decision to make when the band booked a 13-week gig in Wales. By then, he was engaged to be married, and he still had a good job as an apprentice. In the end, the promise of drumming for a living was too good to pass up. He gave up his job and his fiancée, and took off with the band.

It was during this time that bandleader Rory Storm—formerly Alan Caldwell—

suggested that Ritchie adopt a flashier stage name. Together, they came up with "Rings," because of all the chunky rings Ritchie wore on his fingers. That evolved into "Ringo," and Starkey became "Starr" because it sounded better with his new first name. Ringo's onstage drum solos became known as "Starr Time."

In the fall of 1960, Rory Storm and the Hurricanes played in Hamburg, Germany. It was there that Ringo first met—and played with—John, Paul, and George. By then, the boys were known as the Beatles.

In this photo, taken in England sometime around 1960, Rory and the Hurricanes seem to have left their instruments—but not their enthusiasm—behind! That's Ritchie Starkey, soon to become known as Ringo Starr, second from the left.

Chapter 3
Becoming the Beatles

In 1958, two years before he met the Beatles, Ringo Starr was still Ritchie Starkey—and John Lennon, Paul McCartney, and George Harrison were still the Quarrymen. Ritchie was just beginning to discover skiffle and develop his own musical talents. Meanwhile, John and Paul were fine-tuning their songwriting partnership and playing with George and the Quarrymen every chance they got.

The Quarrymen Rock the Casbah

Because John studied at the Liverpool College of Art, which was right around the corner form the Liverpool Institute where Paul and George went to school, the boys began to meet up on their lunch breaks. After they ate lunch, they played and jammed for an hour or two, singing and performing popular tunes of the day for their school chums.

In the evenings and on weekends, they got together to play some more. They also attended concerts, where they studied other musicians' techniques. During the spring and summer of 1958, John and Paul became more serious about their songwriting partnership. They agreed that, from then on, all their songs—whether written together or individually—would always be credited as "Lennon-McCartney."

A number of tunes they wrote during that time later found their way onto Beatles' albums.

Sadly, the Lennon-McCartney partnership was sealed through tragedy. In July 1958, John's mother Julia was hit by a car. She died instantly. John, who had been spending more and more time with his mother since his uncle's death three years earlier, was devastated. Paul was the one person who understood what John was going through, having lost his own mom in 1956. "Now we were both in this; both losing our mothers," said Paul. "This was a bond for us." As Paul had done when his mother died, John used music—along with Paul's understanding—to help him cope with his grief. Many of John's friends believe that, without Paul by his side that summer, John's musical career might have ended with Julia's death.

For the rest of 1958, the Quarrymen continued to practice but rarely performed. While John and Paul focused on songwriting, George became restless. He wanted to keep playing, so he joined three other friends in a band called the Les Stewart Quartet. The Casbah Coffee Club, a new, members-only nightclub for teenagers, hired the quartet to play for its opening night. When two members of the foursome backed out a week before the show, George suggested the Quarrymen take the gig instead.

THE BEATLES

On August 29, 1959, the Quarrymen—joined by Ken Brown, a guitarist from the Les Stewart Quartet—were such a hit at the Casbah that they became the club's resident Saturday night band. Teens lined up by the hundreds to hear the Quarrymen play, even though the band had no drummer. The Quarrymen earned £3 (about $4.70 today) for each performance.

On October 10, 1959, after a dispute over money on the night of their eighth Casbah performance, the Quarrymen walked out of the club—giving up their one regular gig. Ken Brown continued to play at the Casbah with other musicians. A year later, John, Paul, and George returned with a band of a different name.

The Silver Beetles Go to Scotland

Without a drummer, it was tough for the Quarrymen to book concerts. To boost the band's image, and now that Quarry Bank High School was deep in his past, John changed the group's name to Johnny and the Moondogs. Still, the group was making no money and rarely ever performing.

Meanwhile, during the 1959–1960 school year, John was as bored as ever, Paul's grades were falling, and George quit the education system altogether. He took a job at a local department store until he could figure out what to do next with his life.

In January 1960, John's art school friend Stu Sutcliffe sold one of his paintings for a fairly good sum of money. John convinced his mate to spend the cash on a bass guitar and join the band. Stu wasn't a musician, but he figured he

"Hi everyone. Welcome to the Casbah. We're the Quarrymen, and we are going to play you some rock and roll."

John Lennon at the Casbah's opening night

could learn. "And anyway," he told a friend, "the band is going to be the greatest. I want to be part of it."

A few months later, the group changed its name again, this time to honor one of the musicians' heroes, Buddy Holly, who had died in a plane crash a year earlier. Holly's band was called the Crickets. The lads came up with the name the Beetles, but John suggested changing the spelling "to make it look like beat music, just as a joke." They all agreed on the Beatals as the new band name.

The Beatals began rehearsing in the basement of a Liverpool coffee house called the Jacaranda. The owner Allan Williams was impressed with the young band, and he wanted to help the teenaged musicians further their musical careers. He found them a drummer named Tommy Moore. He also arranged for the group—now called the Silver Beetles—to audition to be the back-up band for a rock star named Billy Fury. At the audition, "they blew everyone away," said a musician who

was there. Fury agreed to hire the Silver Beetles, but without Stu Sutcliffe. Fury said Stu was not a good enough bass player. When John refused to go on tour without Stu, the boys lost that job. Instead, they got the big break they longed for with a different artist. In May 1960, the Silver Beetles took to the road for their first-ever tour, as the back-up band for pop star Johnny Gentle.

The two-week circuit through Scotland was badly organized. The musicians had little time to rehearse with Johnny Gentle and little money for food and hotels, and they played in crummy venues. Still, the lads from Liverpool impressed audiences everywhere they performed. They also impressed Johnny Gentle. "I used to watch them work the crowd as though they'd been doing it all their lives, and without any effort other than their amazing talent," he said. "I'd never seen anything like it."

Back to Liverpool

By the time the Silver Beetles returned to Liverpool, the new drummer, Tommy Moore, had had enough of the touring life. He quit, leaving the band drummerless once again. Still, Allan Williams hired the Silver Beetles for a string of Monday night gigs at his Jacaranda club. In August, he booked them into a longer-term engagement at a strip club in Hamburg, Germany, on one condition— they had to find a drummer.

Because they didn't have much work that summer, the Beetles, who had dropped "Silver" from the band name, spent a lot of time hanging around clubs and coffee houses. These included the Casbah, where they had once played. There, they discovered a fantastic new drummer named Pete Best, the son of the club's owner. They asked Pete to join them for the gig in Germany, a job he gladly accepted.

Eager to head to Hamburg, John, Paul, Stu, and Pete quit school (George had already dropped out). They packed up their instruments, organized their passports, and piled into Allan Williams's van. With one final name change, the band—now called the Beatles—hit the road to Hamburg on August 16, 1960.

The Beatles Arrive... in Hamburg

The following night, the band played its first professional gig as the Beatles—but it wasn't exactly under glamorous conditions. The Indra Club, where the teenaged boys performed, was a seedy nightclub in a scary part of Hamburg. The street was lined with strip clubs, run-down cafés, and sleazy bars. At night, the streets filled with drug addicts, prostitutes, and thugs looking for fights. The Beatles slept on mattresses on the floor of a shabby movie theater, where they bathed in filthy restrooms.

In their first few shows, the Beatles were quite stilted, or stiff, onstage. They knew their music and could play a solid set of songs, but they didn't connect with the crowd. Frustrated, the club owner told the guys they had to do better. "*Mach schau!*" he yelled, meaning "make a show of it."

With that, the lads started hamming it up. They jumped around onstage, pretended to sword-fight with each other, danced like gorillas, bonked their heads together, or whatever other silliness they could come up with. They started eating, drinking, and smoking onstage during performances. At first, they deliberately went over the top with their

clowning around, mocking the club owner by overdoing their antics. But the owner—and audiences—loved it. Suddenly, the Indra Club went from being a half-empty seedy nightclub, to a jam-packed seedy nightclub!

Moving on Up

The Indra became so successful that, in October, police shut it down because of noise complaints. The Beatles moved across the street to a slightly more upscale club, the Kaiserkeller. There, they played to crazed crowds for up to 10 hours a night, six nights a week. They alternated sets, or series of songs, with another Liverpool band called Rory Storm and the Hurricanes—whose drummer

Pete Best (seated in front of George, Paul, and John) after being hired on to become the regular drummer for the group that soon began calling itself the Beatles.

happened to be Ringo Starr. "Every night was another amazing jam fest," said Johnny Byrne, the Hurricanes' lead guitarist. "The music got everyone so cranked up, and the whole place just shook like Jell-O."

At the Kaiserkeller, the Beatles played to the rough crowd they had impressed at the Indra, but the Kaiserkeller was also a hangout for artsy students in the area. The group made friends with one particular trio of students, and one of those students particularly appealed to Stu. Astrid Kirchherr was a budding photographer who took early photos of the Beatles. She soon became Stu's girlfriend. He started spending more time with her, and less time with the band. He eventually moved in with Astrid and her mother.

During their Hamburg months, the Beatles changed their look, opting for a tougher image—black leather jackets and pants, pointy shoes, and longer hair. At the same time, they discovered a drug called Preludin, an "upper" that helped them keep their energy up through the grueling performance schedule. They drank heavily, hired prostitutes, stayed up until dawn, and spent what little money they earned.

They also broke the rules of their contract with the Kaiserkeller by performing at another Hamburg club

The Indra Club in Hamburg, where the Beatles got their start in Germany, as it looks today. The club still bills itself as an R&B venue, and its spruced-up exterior includes art that recognizes its place in rock 'n' roll history.

called the Top Ten. When the Kaiserkeller owner found out, he was furious. He fired the Beatles in December. Shortly after that, 17-year-old George was deported for performing underage in nightclubs. Then Paul and Pete were arrested for supposedly setting a fire in the room where they slept. They, too, were deported. Without the rest of the band, there was no reason for John to stay in Hamburg. A few weeks later, he headed back to Liverpool, too, leaving Stu behind with Astrid.

Back in Britain...

The Beatles arrived home from Hamburg tired, discouraged, broke, and "ashamed," said George. Having quit school to follow their big dreams, they all had some explaining to do to their parents.

The fellows went their separate ways for a few weeks before reconnecting for a gig that gave the first hint of what came to be called "Beatlemania." On December 27, 1960, the band played a concert at the Town Hall Ballroom in Litherland, just north of Liverpool. At the time of this concert, Stu was still with Astrid in Germany. Pete's friend, bass player Chas Newby, filled in until Stu returned in January with Astrid.

"The Beatles were an absolute powerhouse, creating an inexplicable and unprecedented frenzy among the spellbound teenagers," wrote Beatles author Mark Lewisohn.

Billed as "Direct from Hamburg," most in the audience assumed the Beatles were German. "We didn't care about that," said John. "It was that evening that we really came out of our

"The Beatles didn't grow up in Liverpool. We grew up in Hamburg."

John Lennon

shell and let go. We stood there being cheered for the first time."

The Beatles had certainly changed since they had left Liverpool four months earlier. They looked different, and they sounded different. They were confident and wildly energetic onstage. John, Paul, George, and Pete agreed this night was a turning point for the Beatles. "Suddenly, we were a wow," said John.

In the audience at the Town Hall Ballroom concert was tour promoter Brian Kelly. Before the Beatles left that night, he booked them for every gig he had available. Suddenly, the Beatles were in demand. During February and March 1961, they played lunchtime and evening concerts at Liverpool's dark and dingy Cavern Club—a huge, underground dance hall. Audiences increased with every show until hundreds of teens crowded into the club to see the lads play. Girls started following the guys everywhere they went. Posters advertised the "Fabulous Beatles," a title that eventually led to their "Fab" nickname.

With so many performances to play, the Beatles needed more musical numbers. They started playing some of their own compositions, including "Like Dreamers Do," "Hold Me Tight," and "Love Me Do." The fans—especially the girls—couldn't get enough of these young, handsome rock 'n' rollers.

Changes Brewing in Hamburg

As successful as the lads had become in Liverpool, they missed the buzz of Hamburg. In April 1961, they returned for a three-month run at the Top Ten, which they had enjoyed because

> *"We were playing for dancing in a hall that could accommodate some 1,500 on the dance floor at one time, but they stopped dancing when we played and surged forward in a crowd to be nearer to us, to watch every movement and above all, to scream. People didn't go to a dance to scream. This was news."*
>
> Drummer Pete Best, talking about the Litherland concert

it was fancier than other clubs they had played in Hamburg. There, they performed with British singer Tony Sheridan.

One day, Stu showed up at the Top Ten with a new hairstyle. Astrid had combed his long hair forward, over his forehead and ears. The others poked fun at him for his new cut, but a few days later, George showed up with the same shaggy look. John, Paul, and Pete laughed at his new hairstyle, so George went back to the old, slicked-back look the next day.

As Stu became more involved with Astrid, he began missing rehearsals. In addition, his musical talent had never really caught up to that of the rest of the boys. Paul felt Stu wasn't committed enough to the band—and it was true. Stu's heart was no longer in it. That summer in Germany, Paul's dislike for Stu became obvious to everyone. One night, the two young men had a fight onstage and, before long, Stu quit the Beatles.

Stu wanted to marry Astrid and stay in Germany to attend art school. Without Stu, the band needed someone on bass.

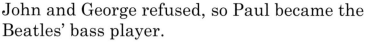

John and George refused, so Paul became the Beatles' bass player.

Just before they left Hamburg that summer, the Beatles got another big break. They were asked to be the back-up band for Sheridan, who was about to make a recording. With Sheridan, the group went temporarily by the name the Beat Brothers. While they were with him, they recorded two songs as a single, "My Bonnie" and "The Saints," in June 1961. The record sold well in Germany. But by the time it was released, the Beatles were home in England where the record didn't get much attention.

Another single recorded by the Beat Brothers/Beatles during their time with Sheridan was an instrumental called "Cry for a Shadow." It was also the only song credited jointly to George Harrison and John Lennon. Even though they recorded it in 1961, the Beatles' label didn't release it until 1964, after their popularity had risen.

When Stu Sutcliffe left the Beatles in 1961, Paul took over playing the bass guitar. Shown here: replicas of a bass guitar played by Paul (left) and a guitar used by George, who was the group's lead guitarist.

Cleaning Up the Act

Back in Liverpool, the Beatles returned to their regular gig at the Cavern Club, packing in audiences for every show. The master of ceremonies, or MC, there encouraged Beatles fans to go to the local record store to buy the single the band had just made with Tony Sheridan.

The shop manager Brian Epstein had never heard of the Beatles and didn't carry the record, but he prided himself on knowing the who's-who in the local music scene.

The Mop Top

In the summer of 1961, Stu's girlfriend Astrid cut and styled his hair into a relaxed, grease-free shape. The others found Stu's new 'do comical—until October, when they adopted the style themselves. For John's 21st birthday, John and Paul took a trip to Paris, where they ran into Jurgen Vollmer who was one of their Hamburg friends. Like many of the artsy students in Hamburg and Paris, Jurgen sported the same shaggy "mod" haircut that Stu wore.

"Jurgen had a flattened down hairstyle with a fringe in the front, which we rather took to," said John. "We went over to his place, and there and then he cut—hacked would be a better word—our hair into the same style." John and Paul returned from Paris with the new look that came to be called the "mop top" (because it looked like a floor mop). George had tried the look months before, but he gave it up when John and Paul made fun of him. Now that his band mates had taken up the look, he combed his hair in the same fashion. The look never worked for Pete because his hair was too curly.

When fans came in asking for "My Bonnie," Brian went to the Cavern Club to find out who the Beatles were and what all the fuss was about. Epstein later recalled:

"It was pretty much an eye-opener to go down into this darkened, dank, smoky cellar in the middle of the day, and to see crowds and crowds of kids watching these four young men on stage. I immediately liked what I heard. They were fresh, and they were honest, and they had what I thought was...star quality."

Brian started attending all the Beatles' concerts and stocking their record in his store. In December 1961, he invited John, Paul, George, and Pete to his office. He offered to be their manager, promising to book them into better venues and get them a recording contract. "Right, then, Brian—manage us," said John.

Immediately, Brian set some ground rules. No more smoking, eating, chewing gum, or drinking onstage. No more shouting at the audience, goofing around with each other, or picking up girls while they were onstage. No more leather pants and jackets—the Beatles were now to wear matching suits and ties. They were to bow at the end of each performance and be on time for every meeting and every show. They were only to play their best songs, and only for an hour at a time.

Brian began promoting the Beatles to the media and working on getting that record deal he had promised. While he was meeting record company producers, the Beatles returned to

Underground Music

When the Quarrymen started their musical careers, they literally played underground. The Casbah Coffee Club, owned by Pete Best's mom Mona, was a members-only dance club for teens, located in the cellar of the Best family's massive home. The Quarrymen painted the walls of the club with stars, dragons, and rainbows. Today, the club has heritage status for its role in the Beatles' development.

The Cavern Club, a transformed underground air-raid shelter, opened in January 1957. The Quarrymen first played there in the late 1950s. The Beatles performed at the Cavern almost 300 times between 1961 and 1963. The sprawling, airless, brick-lined cellar closed in 1973. It reopened in 1991, largely as a tourist attraction.

Mathew Street and the Cavern Club are names that are revered by Beatles fans who visit Liverpool in search of places associated with the early rise of the Fab Four. The original Cavern Club was closed in 1973 and reopened in 1991. The new Cavern Club, shown here on Mathew Street, occupies about 50 percent of the original site. The interior, which replicates the original, was constructed with many of the bricks used in the first club.

Hamburg for a six-week engagement at the fancy new All-Star Club. Astrid Kirchherr, their friend and former band mate Stu Sutcliffe's girlfriend, met them at the airport with terrible news. The night before, Stu had died of a brain hemorrhage (severe bleeding). He was only 21 years old. Though devastated, the band fulfilled its commitment at the All-Star Club, as promised.

When they returned to England, one of the Beatles' first stops was a recording studio in London. After several rejections by other record companies, Epstein had arranged for the band

to audition for producer George Martin at record company EMI's Abbey Road Studios. Martin didn't love the band's music, but he liked the charisma and raw talent of its players. He agreed to sign them to a recording contract—without drummer Pete Best. John, Paul, George, and Brian agreed that Pete was the Beatles' weak link, and they let him go.

In Pete's place, they hired a drummer they had met during their first trip to Hamburg—Ringo Starr of Rory Storm and the Hurricanes. John, Paul, George, and Ringo played together as the Beatles for the first time on August 18, 1962, at a dance back in England. The Fab Four had come together at last.

Beatlemania Sweeps Britain

Now that they had a contract, the lads started recording. In September, they produced "Love Me Do" with "P.S. I Love You" on the flip side. Eventually, it reached #17 on the British record charts. Their next single "Please Please Me," released in January 1963, did considerably better.

As this graffiti-covered street sign suggests, Abbey Road, the location of the first studios to record the Beatles and, later, the name of one of their most famous albums, has become a huge tourist attraction. Because of the graffiti, the sign must be replaced every few weeks!

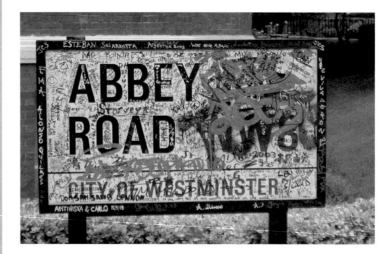

After the band played the song on a British television show, it reached #1 on the charts within a month and became the best-selling record in Britain. Wrote Beatles biographer Bob Spitz:

> *"Up until that time, British rock 'n' roll was basically American music copied—badly—by the British. Now the UK had an innovator of its own. 'Please Please Me' hit the right groove, it was authentic, and it was entirely British."*

Because the Beatles had become so popular, producer George Martin knew the time was right to produce a whole album of songs. John and Paul wrote eight new tunes and, on February 11, 1963, the Beatles recorded a total of 10 songs in just 11 hours! Their first album, titled *Please Please Me*, included "I Saw Her Standing There" and "Do You Want to Know a Secret." After its March release, the album shot to #1 on the charts and stayed there for a record 29 weeks.

Over the next few months, the Beatles became a phenomenon in Britain with three national tours, #1 hit after #1 hit, radio and TV performances, sold-out concerts, and screaming fans following them everywhere.

In October 1963, the British press coined the term "Beatlemania" after a televised concert at the London Palladium. More than 2,000 screaming fans attended the concert, with another 15 million watching on television.

THE FIRST BEATLE BABY

On August 23, 1962, John married his pregnant girlfriend Cynthia Powell. They kept their union a secret to avoid disappointing all the Beatles-crazed girls. Their child, Julian Lennon, was born on April 8, 1963. John was touring with the band so he didn't meet his son until three days later.

Two weeks later, on October 31, about 10,000 fans showed up at London's Heathrow Airport to welcome the band home after its first tour of Sweden. Ground and air traffic were stalled because of the mobs of fans at the airport.

One person stuck in an aircraft, circling the airport while waiting for the crowds to clear so the plane could safely land, was famous American variety show host Ed Sullivan. At that moment, he decided that any band that could cause this much commotion should be on his TV show.

CHARTING MUSICAL SUCCESS— A QUICK PRIMER

Beatles' tunes often topped record charts in the UK, the United States, and Canada. That means that fans loved the music. Record charts rank single songs or albums from most popular to least popular in a given time period. The best position is, of course, #1 on the chart! Most charts list the top 10 or top 100 songs in a week. At the end of the year, many radio stations will "count down" the top 100 or 200 songs of the year, based on sales. In Canada and the United States, *Billboard* magazine's charts are the most esteemed. In Britain, the UK Singles and UK Albums Charts are the most important.

Police struggle to hold back crowds of young fans straining to get closer to the Beatles during one of the Fab Four's appearances in London.

THE MANY "FIFTH BEATLES"

Throughout the Beatles' years together, a number of musicians, assistants, and record industry colleagues contributed to the Fab Four's success. Some performed briefly with the lads, while others helped run the band's business. Some even carried equipment and drove the Beatles to their concerts. Many of these friends-of-the-band have been called "the Fifth Beatle." The term has come to refer to almost anyone who played a secondary—but important—role in the Beatles' rise to fame.

Bass player **Stu Sutcliffe**, John's best friend from art school, was one of the first to be called the Fifth Beatle. Born June 23, 1940, Stuart Fergusson Victor Sutcliffe was the eldest of three children of a ship's engineer and a teacher. As a child, Stu studied piano, sang in his church choir, and played a bit of guitar. As a Beatle, his musical talent never equaled that of his band mates, and his true passion was art. After he left the Beatles, he stayed in Germany with fiancée Astrid Kirchherr and studied at the Hamburg State School of Art for two years. A talented abstract painter, Stu was considered one of the school's best students. Since his death on April 10, 1962, Stu's artwork has been shown in almost 40 exhibitions around the world—including about 25 solo shows.

Born November 24, 1941, in India (which was then under British rule), drummer **Pete Best** was another early Fifth Beatle. Pete's biological father died during World War II. His mother Mona married military officer and boxing champ Johnny Best in 1944. At the end of 1945, the family (which then included Pete's little brother Rory) traveled by

In 1964, during the Beatles' first world tour, Ringo Starr became ill. The lads hired drummer Jimmie Nicol (left photo, standing at right) to sit in until Ringo was well enough to rejoin the band. American organist and singer Billy Preston (shown in right photo with George in 1974) played with the Beatles when they recorded as a group and as solo artists.

ship to Liverpool, where Mona opened the Casbah Coffee Club. There, Pete played drums with a group called the Blackjacks, until Paul McCartney asked him to join the Beatles in 1960. Two years later, when he was dismissed from the band, Pete's fans were outraged. For weeks, they heckled the Beatles with jeers of "Pete forever, Ringo never!" For a few years, Pete drummed for other unsuccessful bands, but he soon quit music to become a civil servant. In 1988, he returned to his roots and formed the Pete Best Band, which continues to perform today.

Another person considered a Fifth Beatle was the band's manager **Brian Epstein**. He was born in Liverpool on September 19, 1934, the eldest child of a well-to-do businessman and his wife. After rejecting a career in the family's furniture store, he briefly joined the military before trying out acting school. When that didn't work out, he rejoined the family business, which by then included a music store. Eventually, Brian became very successful managing the family-owned record store, which was just down the street from the Cavern Club. That's where he first saw the Beatles and recognized that they would be "bigger than Elvis." Under his management, the Beatles shot to fame—and became very wealthy. Brian stayed out of the artistic side of the Beatles' business, but almost single-handedly organized their business affairs, arranging contracts, merchandise deals, and tour schedules for six years until his death from a drug overdose in 1967.

Record producer **George Martin** has also been known as a Fifth Beatle. Now in his 80s, George is a trained musician who studied classical piano and oboe in his youth. He retired from record producing in 1998, after almost 50 years on the job. When he first met the Beatles, he agreed to take a chance on them, even though they were still completely unknown at the time. He liked them, personally, almost more than he liked their music when he first heard it! Over the years, he wrote and sometimes even played musical arrangements for many Beatles songs. He offered expertise, imagination, and technical advice, but his greatest skill may have been knowing when to step in and when to leave the Beatles to be their creative selves.

Manager Brian Epstein (left) and recording producer George Martin were responsible for key components of the Beatles' success story.

Chapter 4
The Beatles Define a Generation

Afew days after the fan frenzy at Heathrow Airport, the Beatles became the first "long-haired boys" to perform for members of the British Royal Family. The band's arrival at the Royal Variety Show on November 4, 1963, drew more excitement than the entrance of royalty! It was at this concert that John Lennon famously said to the crowd: "For our last number, I'd like to ask your help. Would the people in the cheaper seats clap your hands? And the rest of you, if you'll just rattle your jewelry." After the performance, the Queen Mother (the mother of Queen Elizabeth II), pronounced the Beatles "so fresh and vital. I simply adore them." Clearly, she wasn't the only one who felt that way.

Beatlemania Crosses the Atlantic
It wasn't long before the Beatles' mind-boggling surge to stardom in the UK, along with news of their historic royal performance, caught the attention of international media. When 15-year-old Marsha Albert of suburban Washington, D.C., watched CBS News's December 10, 1963, story about the Fab Four, she wrote to local radio station WWDC and asked, "Why can't we have music like that here in America?" It was in response to this letter that DJ Carroll James

THE BEATLES

arranged for a flight attendant on BOAC airlines (now British Airways) to hand deliver to him a copy of "I Want to Hold Your Hand."

Because Marsha had been the listener to request the Beatles' song, Carroll invited her to introduce it on the radio. He wrote the script, and Marsha read it into a microphone: "Ladies and gentlemen, for the first time on the air in the United States, here are the Beatles singing 'I Want To Hold Your Hand.'" As soon as they heard the sound of the lads from Liverpool, listeners called the station, requesting the song over and over again. They also flooded their local record stores looking to buy copies of it.

By then, variety show host Ed Sullivan had booked the Beatles for three appearances on his show for the following February. Armed with those bookings—and the fan demand for Beatles' music—manager Brian Epstein convinced

FOR THE RECORD...

WWDC's presentation of "I Want to Hold Your Hand" may not, in fact, have been the first time a Beatles song was played on radio in the United States. A number of other American stations have also claimed to have been the first to play Beatles' music in the United States—including WFRX in West Frankfort, Illinois. At the time, George Harrison's sister Louise lived in a nearby town. In spring 1963, her mother sent her a copy of "From Me to You." Louise took the record to WFRX, which played it in June 1963. In September of the same year, George visited his sister in Illinois. He took a copy of "She Loves You" to WFRX. The radio station played that one, too— three months before Carroll James played "I Want to Hold Your Hand" over the Washington, D.C., airwaves.

FOR THE RECORD...

NBC was the first television network to present the Beatles to ar
audience. It showed a short clip of the band on the *Huntley-Brin*
November 18, 1963. CBS aired its five-minute story the mornin
22 and planned to repeat it on the evening news. Later that day
President John F. Kennedy was assassinated and all other progra
canceled. CBS finally replayed the Beatles story on December 1(

The first variety show host to present the Beatles to a U.S. te
was Ed Sullivan's rival Jack Paar. On January 3, 1964, Paar aired
recorded in England—of the Beatles singing "She Loves You." Tha
month before the Beatles' first live television performance in the
on Sullivan's show.

Capitol Records in the United States to release
"I Want To Hold Your Hand" immediately. It
had been scheduled for a late-January release.
On December 26, 1963, the single hit American
record stores and sold more than 250,000 copies
in three days. In mid-January, the song started
a 15-week run on the record charts in the United
States, reaching #1 on February 1. It held the
top spot for seven weeks, until it was replaced
by another Beatles song, "She Loves You."

Throughout January 1964, Capitol Records
flooded the market with promotional items—
Beatles wigs, buttons, stickers, and T-shirts that
proclaimed "The Beatles Are Coming!" They
were designed to add to the Beatles buzz already
sweeping across America. The lads' first U.S.
album *Meet the Beatles!* sold more than 750,000
copies in one week after its January 20 release.
By the time the band landed in New York on
February 7, 1964, thousands of screaming fans
were on hand to greet the Fab Four.

A Classic Portrait

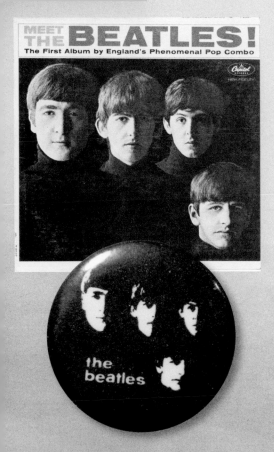

Meet the Beatles! came out in January 1964. The first U.S. Beatles album released by Capitol Records, it was based on *With the Beatles,* which had already been released in the UK and Canada. The cover photo, as initially conceived in the UK, was to stand by itself, with no words. The recording company vetoed the idea, however, because they didn't feel the group was famous enough to have the photo stand on its own. The company also didn't care for the image because the lads weren't smiling, but producer George Martin intervened and cleared the way to use it. The stark, black-and-white image has been reproduced on many T-shirts, posters, and Beatles souvenirs from the 1960s, including the button shown here.

It was "a teen-age storm," wrote one reporter. The British Invasion of the United States had begun.

On Top of the World

On February 9, 1964, the Beatles made their first of three appearances on *The Ed Sullivan Show.* About 50,000 fans applied for 728 studio seats, and 73 million people—or one-third of the

"We knew that America would make us or break us as world stars. In fact, she made us."

Brian Epstein

U.S. population—watched the band's American television debut. Said Sullivan:

"I had never seen any scenes to compare with the bedlam that was occasioned by their debut [on the show]... Broadway was jammed with people for almost eight blocks. [Fans] screamed, yelled, and stopped traffic. It was indescribable... There has never been anything like it in show business."

A week later, the Fab Four appeared on Sullivan's show again, this time live from Miami, in front of an audience of 3,500 people, with 70 million viewers at home. Between the two Sullivan shows, the Beatles also performed for 20,000 fans at the Washington Coliseum and two full houses at New York's Carnegie

THE BEATLES

The Beatles upon their arrival at John F. Kennedy International Airport on February 7, 1964. Two days later, they faced screaming crowds on the first of many appearances on The Ed Sullivan Show.

Hall. They left New York on February 22, the day before their pre-taped third Sullivan performance went on the air.

The next few months were a whirlwind of activity for John, Paul, George, and Ringo. As soon as they returned to England, they recorded the album *A Hard Day's Night*—their first collection of all-original songs. Immediately after that, they acted in their first feature film, also called *A Hard Day's Night*. In April, Beatles' songs held the top five spots on *Billboard* magazine's singles chart in the United States. At the same time, their albums took positions #1 and #2 on the album charts. This amazing chart-topping feat has never been repeated!

Next up for the Fab Four was a quick tour of Europe, followed by 32 concerts in 19 days in Australia and New Zealand. By that time, the strain of fame had started to wear the lads down.

A Note Worth Noting

Before their first appearance on *The Ed Sullivan Show*, the Beatles received a stack of notes welcoming them to the United States. When Paul read one special message, a huge smile crossed his face. The note said, "Congratulations on your appearance on the Ed Sullivan Show and your visit to America. We hope your engagement will be a successful one and your visit pleasant." It was signed, "Elvis."

Paul, George, John, and Ringo rehearse before their appearance on The Ed Sullivan Show.

Ed Sullivan—A Sunday Night Staple

The longest-running television variety show in U.S. history (1948–1971), *The Ed Sullivan Show* presented the most important musical and comedy acts of its day. The Beatles' first performance on the show remains one of the highest-rated TV moments of all time. Elvis Presley, the Jackson 5, the Doors, the Supremes, and the Rolling Stones also gave career-changing performances on Sullivan's Sunday evening stage, as did comedians such as Carol Burnett, Joan Rivers, Richard Pryor, and Phyllis Diller. Even Kermit the Frog got his start on *The Ed Sullivan Show*! The key to Sullivan's success was his ability to spot up-and-coming talent—and to present something for every age group, so the whole family could watch the show together.

During an era when few African Americans were able to find steady gigs on television, Ed Sullivan (shown at top) gave national prominence to dozens of black entertainers every Sunday night on his show. The Supremes (shown left during a 1966 performance on the show) were a special favorite of Sullivan and appeared on his show 15 times. The Jackson 5 (shown during their own TV special in 1972) made their first appearance on The Ed Sullivan Show *in 1969. (That's Michael in the center!)*

When they performed, they couldn't even hear themselves play because of all the screaming fans. They couldn't go outside on their own without being mobbed. That meant, when they toured, they were confined to hotel suites, cars, and backstage dressing rooms. "It's like we're four freaks being wheeled out to be seen, shake our hair about, and get back in our cage afterwards," said John.

At one tour stop in Melbourne, Australia, more than 100 police officers, soldiers, and volunteers tried to hold back 250,000 screaming fans who wanted to get close to their idols. The security force failed, the crowd surged, women fainted, and many fans were trampled. Ambulances carried 100 people to the hospital that day. Another time, Ringo was injured by mobbing fans.

Great fame was something the Beatles had wanted, but nobody could have predicted this level of international celebrity—or how quickly the lads had achieved it. Remember, they had only released their first single 20 months earlier!

was the same everywhere. Crowds of kids,
..., screaming and fainting, battling through
... to touch their beloved Beatles. As for the
...lves, lasting a scant thirty-one minutes, they
...ting inside a funnel cloud. The four Beatles
...h onstage, unannounced, clutching their
... like body armor while flashbulbs exploded
...nd them in a hail of blinding light."

Beatles biographer Bob Spitz

The movie *A Hard Day's Night* came out in early July 1964 to rave reviews from fans, critics, and the Beatles themselves. "I dug *A Hard Day's Night*," said John. "We knew it was better than other rock movies, though not as good as James Bond."

In August 1964, the Fab Four arrived in the United States for their first full tour of that country, with additional stops in Toronto and Montreal in Canada. They performed 32 shows in 24 cities in 34 days, greeted by thousands of screaming fans at every venue. The Beatles pocketed a record $1 million for that concert circuit.

BANKING ON THE BEATLES

The Beatles weren't the only ones who profited from their fame. One hotel owner sold unwashed bed linen after the Fab Four had slept on it. The businessmen who bought the linen cut it into small squares and sold each piece for $10. Someone else chopped up the towels the lads had used to wipe their faces after a concert and sold the sweaty bits of cloth. Fans even offered to purchase bottles of the Beatles' bathwater or used shaving foam.

The Hard Day's Night Hotel, named after the song, album, and movie of the same name, is the only Beatles-themed hotel in the world. Located in the Beatles' hometown of Liverpool, the hotel features statues of each of the Fab Four lining the front of its 19th-century building. Here, the statue of John flashes a peace sign from its perch overlooking, appropriately enough, the corner of Mathew and John Streets!

By the end of the year, they had released 10 albums and 15 singles in the UK, the United States, and Canada.

Meeting the Queen—and the King

For John, Paul, George, and Ringo, 1965 was much the same as 1964—another tour of Britain, another tour of Europe, another tour of the United States, another performance on *The Ed Sullivan Show*, another meeting with Bob Dylan, and another feature film.

UNDER THE INFLUENCE... OF DYLAN

If there were drawbacks to the Beatles' great celebrity, there were also great perks. One privilege they enjoyed was meeting all their musical heroes—including folk legend Bob Dylan. Many have argued that the downside of that meeting was that he introduced the young men to a new illegal substance. To that point, alcohol and "uppers" had been the Beatles' drugs of choice. But, after their 1964 meeting with Dylan, they also became frequent smokers of marijuana, or pot.

Clearly on the upside, Dylan influenced them musically. The Beatles' sound became more mature and thoughtful after their time with the folk singer. "Vocally, and poetically, Dylan was a huge influence," said Paul. Similarly, the lads from Liverpool influenced Dylan's sound. His music shifted from a "pure" form of folk music, accompanied by harmonica and acoustic guitar, to a style that incorporated rock 'n' roll and made use of back-up musicians and electronically amplified instruments.

In the 1960s, the lines between politics and poetry, and folk music and rock 'n' roll, often blended and blurred. Here, music legend Bob Dylan, who influenced the Beatles and was influenced by them, is shown at the civil rights March on Washington in 1963. He is with fellow folk singer Joan Baez, who was an important part of the civil rights and anti-Vietnam War movements.

THE BRITISH ARE COMING!

The Beatles' performances on *The Ed Sullivan Show* introduced American music lovers to the British beat for the first time. The show appearances also opened the door to a musical time period known as the British Invasion. For three years, British bands rushed to the United States, where they took over American record charts. Some of the most famous bands to cross the Atlantic Ocean at that time were the Rolling Stones, the Dave Clark Five, the Animals, the Kinks, Gerry and the

Pacemakers, Herman's Hermits, and the Hollies. British movies, actors, fashion, and fashion models also became popular in America during this time.

Two of the most popular groups at the time of the British Invasion were the Rolling Stones and the Dave Clark Five. The Stones, shown top left in a *Billboard* magazine ad—that's Mick Jagger on the right—had a sound that clearly showed its American R&B roots. They also projected a rough, "shaggy" image. Following their first appearance on *The Ed Sullivan Show* in 1964, on which they sang their hit single "Time Is on My Side," Sullivan was critical of their appearance and swore he would never hire them again. As it turned out, he did have them back, at least five more times! The Dave Clark Five are shown bottom left with Sullivan in 1964. This photo was probably taken at the time they performed their hit "Glad All Over" during the first of their numerous appearances on his show. The DC5 had a somewhat harder-driving sound than the Beatles, but they cultivated a look that was, if anything, even more clean-cut than that of the Fab Four!

The lads traveled to the Bahamas, Austria, and rural England for their second movie *Help!* Like *A Hard Day's Night*, this film was a comedy with a silly plot—but the fellows didn't enjoy making this one as much as they had enjoyed the first movie. They felt *Help!* was more work than fun. To help them cope (or so they thought), they used marijuana. They smoked so much that they were stoned, or drugged, for most of the film shoot. Because of this, they ruined scenes by giggling uncontrollably, and they couldn't remember their lines. Scenes took a very long time to film.

A 2007 photo of a bus in Liverpool promoting tourism with a larger-than-life portrait of the Fab Four. The group portrait first appeared on the album Beatles for Sale, *which was initially released in the UK in 1964. The album was not officially released in the United States until 1987. During the 23 years between the two releases, British copies of the album popped up in the United States, and other Beatles albums carried songs from* Beatles for Sale.

In April, John and George discovered another mind-altering drug called LSD, when a friend slipped it into their coffee without their knowledge. Before long, the two became regular users. John's 1966 song "Dr. Robert" is said to be about his introduction to, and use of, LSD. "Take a drink from this special cup," the song says. Paul and Ringo also admitted to trying LSD on occasion.

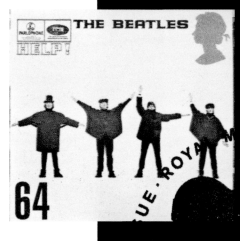

This album cover for Help!, *as depicted on a British postage stamp, shows the Fab Four imitating a series of nonsensical semaphore flag symbols.*

Two months later, suggestions of drug use again helped create a negative image of the Beatles when they attended a historic royal event, reportedly under the influence of marijuana. In June, the Beatles became the first-ever musicians to receive the title of MBE, or Member of the Order of the British Empire. According to John, prior to Queen Elizabeth II bestowing the honor on the Fab Four before a stately gathering at Buckingham Palace, the boys smoked pot in the washroom. George and Paul later maintained that they had smoked regular tobacco, not marijuana. But John's story, which arose from interviews he had with *Rolling Stone* magazine in 1970, has understandably been the one that most people have heard. Even without that allegation, the boys' appointment offended past MBE honorees. Most of them were military heroes who felt rock musicians weren't worthy of such a distinction.

The lads were also high when they met their idol Elvis Presley in August 1965, although their condition was unlikely to cause as much of a fuss with Elvis as it might have with the Royal Family. During a rare break from touring, the Fab Four met the King—Elvis—at his home in Bel Air, California. It was a private meeting, with no photos or recording allowed. The Beatles were said to have arrived "stoned and star struck," and the historic three-hour get-together was reportedly awkward for everyone. The five musicians jammed a bit, played pool, and chatted—and never got together again.

While Elvis's reign over the music world was on the decline by that point, the Beatles were just gearing up. On August 15, the Fab Four performed a concert considered a turning point in their careers, and for the concert scene in general. The venue was New York's Shea Stadium, home to the New York Mets baseball team from 1964 to 2008. Almost 56,000 fans, the Beatles' biggest audience ever, crowded into the ballpark to see the lads from Liverpool. It was the first major outdoor rock 'n' roll concert anywhere in the world, and the band took home a world-record $160,000 for the 30-minute performance. It is considered to be the concert that launched the rock-concert-as-event kind of spectacle we still see today. "This is when the Beatles stopped being teen pop stars and became legends," said one writer.

The Perils of Popularity

In many ways, the Shea Stadium concert was exhilarating for the band. After all, all those people were there to see *them*! In other ways, though, it was a disturbing experience. The streets of New York were impossibly congested because of their visit, so the Beatles traveled by

This Paul pin was originally part of a set of four Beatles buttons issued in 1964. It has been separated from its mates for several decades!

helicopter to a landing site near the ballpark. There, they climbed into waiting armored cars that shuttled them to the stadium. Then they had to run through a tunnel to get to the stage to avoid being mobbed. "It was organized like a military operation," said a photographer who was with the band at the time.

Inside the stadium, an 8-foot (2.5-meter) fence separated the stands and the fans from the ball field. About 2,000 police and security officers patrolled a 100-foot (30-m) expanse of grass between the fence and the stage to make sure nobody got too close to the band. Still, fans launched themselves over the fence throughout the concert, only to be tackled and removed by security.

As for the music, John said later, "It was ridiculous—we couldn't hear ourselves sing." During the last two numbers, he admitted, he and George weren't even playing their guitars. "We were just messing about." From this concert on, the band became increasingly dissatisfied with performing for fans who screamed so much that neither the Beatles nor the audience could hear the music.

By the end of 1965, the Beatles had added five albums and seven singles to their discography (list of recordings). That was half the number they had produced the previous year. One of those singles, "Yesterday," written and sung solo by Paul McCartney, has gone on to become the most recorded song in

Young fans climb a fence in New York's Shea Stadium to get closer to the Beatles during the Fab Four's August 15, 1965, concert. The screams of the largest crowd ever to see a rock concert at that time were so deafening, that not even the Beatles themselves could hear their music. The concert lasted only 30 minutes.

FAMILY TIES

In 1964, John Lennon's absentee father showed up at his son's home, almost 20 years after they had last seen each other. Over the next few months, John gave Alf money and bought him a house, while Alf sold his life story to a gossip magazine and married a woman 30 years his junior. Before long, John realized that his father only wanted money and he kicked Alf out of his life for good. In 1965, John bought a new house for his Aunt Mimi. Until then, she had still lived in the same Liverpool house where she had raised John. There, fans camped out on her front lawn, sometimes even stealing things they thought John might have touched. She needed to get away. Her new home in southern England was 265 miles (426 km) from Liverpool.

THE BEATLES 'TOONS

In fall 1965, at the height of their popularity, the Fab Four began a series of weekly TV appearances—as cartoon characters! The Beatles' half-hour Saturday morning show featured two short cartoon episodes, each named for a Beatles song, with a sing-along segment in between. The 39 episodes were co-produced by animation studios in the United States, Canada, the UK, Australia, and the Netherlands. The real-life Beatles had nothing to do with the show. Two actors—one American, one British—did the four voices.

The show was a hit with audiences. At first, the human Beatles said they weren't all that enthusiastic about their animated twins, but they eventually grew to like the cartoons. "They were so bad or silly that they were good, if you know what I mean," George said 30 years later.

This cartoon version of the Beatles appears on a jukebox from the 1960s.

history. More than 3,000 different versions of "Yesterday" have been recorded by artists from around the globe. In 1999 and 2000, BBC radio, MTV, and *Rolling Stone* magazine all named "Yesterday" the best song of the 20th century. This song is also considered to be the debut of Paul's solo writing career. Until that time, he and John had collaborated on almost every song. Even though the credits for "Yesterday" list Lennon and McCartney as the writers—as do all Beatles recordings—this one was Paul's.

As they moved into 1966, the Beatles' sound was evolving—becoming deeper, moodier, more poetic and tender, and sometimes even angry. The musicians began experimenting with different instruments. For example, the song "Norwegian Wood" on *Rubber Soul*—1965's final album—featured George playing an instrument from India called a sitar.

As the Beatles' music changed, so did the relationships among the men. Conflict started to creep into the group, as John and Paul began to clash personally and creatively.

The 1966 Revolver *album featured such notable Beatles songs as "Yellow Submarine," "Good Day Sunshine," and "Eleanor Rigby." In June and July, around the time when songs on the album were being released, the Beatles were on tour in Asia. They didn't play any songs from the album on that tour, though, or on what would be their final U.S. tour in August. The omission of this album from these tours was a sign of how far their work had progressed in technical sophistication.*

WEDDING BELLS

In February 1965, Ringo Starr married his longtime girlfriend Maureen Cox. The two had met at the Cavern Club in 1962, just after Ringo had started playing with the Beatles. The couple's first child Zak was born in September 1965.

In January 1966, George married Pattie Boyd, who was a model he had met two years earlier while filming *A Hard Day's Night*. Paul, the only remaining bachelor Beatle, was George's best man.

In 1966, to add the fuel to the fire, the Beatles made several public relations blunders that put a strain on the band and its connection to the public.

Bigger Than Who?

For the first few months of 1966, John, Paul, George, and Ringo went their separate ways for a much-needed break. During that time, British reporter Maureen Cleave interviewed John for the *London Evening Standard*. Among other things, she asked him for his take on religion. He said, "Christianity will go. It will vanish and shrink… [The Beatles are] more popular than Jesus now."

The article appeared shortly after the interview, without any fuss. But John's words came back to haunt him the next summer—subjecting the band to widespread criticism and boycotts, and the boys to personal risk.

The Beatles as Butchers?

Meanwhile, the lads took to the photo studio to shoot a cover picture for their next album, *The Beatles Yesterday And Today*. In the cover photo, the four of them are wearing butchers' coats and are draped in raw meat and beheaded baby dolls. For the photographer, the photo was a social statement—something to do with idol-worship, while showing that the idols were actually flesh-and-blood people. For the public, though, the photo was considered simply tasteless.

The infamous "butcher" cover of The Beatles Yesterday And Today *album.*

When the album came out in June, the cover drew such outrage that most copies were recalled the next day. At first, the album was re-released with a different cover shot pasted over the original. Very quickly, fans discovered they could peel the new picture off to reveal the original "butcher" photo beneath. Once again, the album was recalled and new album covers were made. Not surprisingly, copies of the original meat-and-doll album cover have become collector's items selling for thousands of dollars each.

A Holy Mess!

In June 1966, the Beatles set out on another tour—this time to Japan and the Philippines. For the first time in their careers, they received negative receptions at their tour stops. In Japan, they received death threats from a group of people who believed that the concert venue was a sacred place and the Beatles shouldn't be allowed to play there. In the Philippines, First Lady Imelda Marcos expected the Fab Four at a reception at the Presidential Palace. The musicians had no idea they were supposed to be there, but to Imelda—and her citizens—

DID YOU KNOW?

John was known as "the smart Beatle," Paul was "the cute Beatle," George was "the quiet Beatle," and Ringo was "the funny Beatle."

their no-show was considered a serious snub.
From that moment on, ill will, insults, and
violence greeted them everywhere they went
in the Philippines.

At the end of July, just before the Beatles
returned to the United States for their third
North American tour, what has become known
as John's "bigger than Jesus" comment came
back to haunt the lads. An American magazine
reprinted part of the original British newspaper
article, taking his words out of context. Readers
took offense, especially in more conservative
parts of the South.

DJs refused to play Beatles records and
encouraged their listeners to boycott the band
and its music. One DJ found a machine to shred
Beatles records and encouraged listeners to
bring him their albums to destroy. In another
community, a pastor organized a Beatles bonfire
to burn records and memorabilia. Meanwhile,
John explained that his comments were
directed toward a discussion that had long gone
on concerning the decline of Christianity in the
UK, and not toward the United States, which
was far from his mind when he said that. Even
after this and a somewhat frustrated-sounding
apology for having said anything in the first
place, Beatles bans continued—and not just in
the United States. In Spain, the Netherlands,
and South Africa, radio stations were forbidden
to play Beatles songs. All four Beatles received
death threats.

In the end, while the 14-city North American
tour (13 U.S. cities and one in Toronto in
Canada) was mostly successful, audiences
were generally smaller than in previous years.

Also, because of the "Jesus" comment, there was tension in the air at every stop. It proved to be the last straw for the Beatles.

Given the hostility they had met in Japan, the Philippines, and the United States, the fact that they couldn't leave their hotel rooms without being mobbed by fans, and the reality that they no longer enjoyed performing, the Beatles decided their 1966 North American tour would be their last. On August 29, at Candlestick Park in San Francisco, after performing 1,400 concerts in four years, the Beatles played their final show for paying fans.

That's not to say they no longer made music. In fact, the Beatles were about to make what is considered the greatest album of their careers. At the same time, though, tragedy and continuing conflict were soon to spell the end for the band.

An amused-looking Paul is helped through a crowd of excited fans in London on July 8, 1966. About a month later, the lads faced a less welcoming reception from many Americans following John's comments about the popularity of the Beatles and Jesus in the UK.

Chapter 5
The Studio Years, The Final Years

After the final San Francisco concert, the Beatles went their separate ways for a few months. George went to India to study sitar music, Paul wrote a film score, Ringo took a vacation, and John played a small role in a movie. Because he portrayed a military man in the film, John had to cut off his signature mop top hair. His new 'do, combined with the fact that the group was suddenly out of the public eye, sparked rumors that the band was splitting up. In reality, they were growing up—musically and individually.

Sgt. Pepper and the Summer of Love

Since they were no longer touring, the Beatles now had time to experiment in the recording studio. Rather than quickly bashing out albums as they had done a few years earlier, they finally had the luxury to create elaborate projects that were far ahead of their time in terms of technical brilliance.

With the arrival of four-track recording (versus the two tracks, or layers, of the past), the musicians could mix together many different sounds. They added tricks such as slowing down or speeding up selected parts of tracks, looping musical phrases over and over again, and playing tapes backward.

They brought in sound effects, electronic noises, and other musicians—40 symphony musicians at one point. Wrote biographer Bob Spitz:

"Recording was no longer just a way of putting out songs, but a new way of creating them... [They were] producing amazing results. There was a sense of real adventure—and real accomplishment—in the studio."

The resulting recordings were so complex, the songs could not have been presented live in concert, even if the Beatles had wanted to continue touring.

In June 1967, the Beatles released what *Rolling Stone* magazine later named as the "most important' record album of all time—*Sgt. Pepper's Lonely Hearts Club Band*. To produce it, the Beatles spent 700 hours over a five-month period in the studio. It was the first-ever rock album to include liner notes and lyrics. It was also the first-ever rock album to be marketed with short promotional films, films that helped pave the way for the music videos of today. "By packaging the album the way they did, the Beatles were the first music group to present rock 'n' roll music as an art form," wrote author Bruce Glassman.

The album's cover photo featured images of dozens of celebrated actors, artists, authors, sports figures, spiritual leaders, and even former Beatle Stu Sutcliffe. It has become a visual symbol of the 1960s. The album outsold anything the Beatles had done before, selling 2.5 million copies in its first three months on the market.

At the time the album was released, the world was in upheaval. The youth of Europe and North America were questioning the moral, ethical, and philosophical fabric of Western society. They embraced freedom and rejected their parents' value systems, which they believed were outdated. "Peace" and "make love not war" were the themes of the day. Hippies, drug use, anti-war protests, and all things psychedelic were everywhere. During that summer of 1967, the music, values, and lifestyles of young people became a kind of centerpiece for the greater wave of change that took hold during the 1960s. That summer became known as "the summer of love." The Beatles album *Sgt. Pepper's Lonely Hearts Club Band* was its songbook.

With that album, John, Paul, George, and Ringo cast aside their cute mop top haircuts and spiffy suits in favor of long hair, mustaches, and loose, colorful outfits. They inspired a whole

One of the most recognized, imitated, and talked-about album covers in the history of recorded music—the cover of Sgt. Pepper's Lonely Hearts Club Band. *Its collage of famous people, living and dead, includes two versions of the Beatles themselves. All of the "guests" on the cover appear gathered for an event that many felt resembled a graveside funeral service. When viewed that way, the cover made some people think that it was predicting the breakup of the Beatles. Others saw it more positively, as the passing on of the "old" Beatles in favor of a group defined by the day-glo colors of their uniforms and the psychedelic contents of their songs.*

new kind of Beatlemania. Fans now looked to the quartet as musical geniuses, poets, and philosophers. What the Beatles' adoring fans didn't know at this point, though, was that a personal and professional rift between John and Paul was starting to drive the Beatles apart.

A Blow to the Band

During his visit to India in 1966, George had become interested in Eastern religions. To share his newfound spirituality, he persuaded his fellow Beatles and their wives or girlfriends to attend a weekend-long meditation workshop in August 1967. After all, they could use some peace and quiet after the whirlwind of the past few years!

While they were at the retreat in Wales, they received news that Brian Epstein, their longtime manager, had overdosed on sleeping pills and died. The Beatles were shocked and devastated.

A postage stamp from Laos shows the Beatles at their Apple offices in London during the launch of Sgt. Pepper's Lonely Hearts Club Band *in June 1967.*

FOR THE RECORD...

A drawing by John's son inspired one of the Beatles' most famous songs, "Lucy in the Sky with Diamonds." Julian drew the picture of "a dark blue sky with some very rough looking stars" at nursery school one day. In the corner was a stick-figure image of his friend Lucy O'Donnell. When he showed the picture to his dad, Julian said, "That's Lucy in the sky, you know, with diamonds."

Many fans believed the song was about drugs because the initials of its title words spelled LSD. LSD is a drug that causes people to hallucinate, or see things that aren't there. While this song wasn't about drugs, other Beatles songs were. Paul said, "Got To Get You Into My Life" (1966) was about marijuana, and the entire *Sgt. Pepper's Lonely Hearts Club Band* album was "a drug album." He said the Beatles were using drugs during the entire writing and recording process. But he also pointed out that drug use was so common at that time that it was easy to attach drug references to all sorts of song lyrics.

Recalling Their Roots

Two famous singles released in February 1967, and later included on the Beatles' *Magical Mystery Tour* album, drew from the young men's memories of Liverpool. "Strawberry Fields Forever" was named for a children's home called Strawberry Field (no "s"). When John was a boy, he could see the orphanage from his window at Aunt Mimi's house. He often played there and attended garden parties on the grounds. The song "Penny Lane" was named after a real street near the homes of John and Paul. The two lads used to meet at Penny Lane to catch a bus to downtown Liverpool.

The 32-year-old's death was ruled accidental, but some people believe he killed himself. Because the Beatles were no longer touring, Brian had been feeling more and more lost. The last six years of his life had been about promoting the Beatles and organizing their tours, public appearances, and media coverage. Now he had nothing much to do when it came to the band. He was depressed and not sleeping well. He thought the lads didn't need him any more.

For the Beatles, that was far from the truth. Without him, their world was about to fall apart. "The Beatles were finished when Eppy died," said John. "I knew, deep inside me, that that was it. Without him, we'd had it."

None of the lads had any idea how to run the business side of things—a business that was, by now, a multimillion-dollar empire. They didn't have Brian's business knowledge, his ability to manage money, or the know-how to put together a contract. Other managers tried to step in, but

The entrance to Strawberry Field, an orphanage in Liverpool, England. It shows the graffiti left by the many fans who have visited the entrance over the years to get a glimpse of the place where John Lennon remembered playing as a young boy—the place that inspired the Beatles' 1967 hit song "Strawberry Fields Forever."

the Beatles didn't want them. "Without Brian Epstein to control and direct it, this larger-than-life entity known as 'the Beatles' was like an automobile without a driver careening down a highway at high speed," wrote author Bill Yenne.

Another role Brian had played, without the Beatles even knowing it, was managing their relationships with each other. Without Brian's calming presence and his ability to soothe bruised egos, John, Paul, George, and Ringo struggled to continue working as a team. Their bickering and disagreements became more frequent and more serious.

Magic or Tragic?

When Paul tried to step in to fill Brian's shoes, the others resented his efforts at leadership. "Paul took over and supposedly led us," said John. "But what is leading us when we went round in circles?"

Still, the others went along with Paul when he came up with the idea of taking a "magical mystery tour," as a way of getting their minds off their friend's death. The plan was to travel around Britain in a brightly painted bus, stopping wherever they felt like it, playing music, and filming silly antics to make a movie. They had no plan, no director, and no script. They made it up as they went along—and it showed in the final product.

In December 1967, the *Magical Mystery Tour* movie aired on BBC television. Critics called the 52-minute film "appalling," "worse than terrible," and "rubbish, piffle, chaotic, flop, tasteless..." You get the idea. Even the Beatles realized it was a disaster. "There was no plot," said Paul, while John called it "the most expensive home movie ever."

The album of the same name was more successful. In the United States, it stayed at #1 on the charts for eight weeks and was nominated for a Grammy Award for best album of 1968. It included many hit singles, including the title song, "Strawberry Fields," "Penny Lane," and "All You Need Is Love." In recent years, Paul has thrilled thousands of fans in stadiums and arenas worldwide with "Hello, Goodbye" as his opening number on tour.

In their efforts to take control of the business side of the Beatles after Brian's death, the band founded a collection of companies called Apple Corps. It included Apple Records, Apple Publishing, Apple Films, Apple Electronics, and Apple Retail, a clothing boutique. Unfortunately, the store was disorganized and badly run. It opened in December 1967 and closed seven months later. The other businesses in the Apple Corps group were equally badly run. Most of them, except for Apple Records, also eventually failed because of financial and legal problems.

Seeking Peace, Finding Creativity

In the spring of 1968, to escape the grind of their lives and make peace with losing their friend Brian, the Beatles decided to spend three months at an ashram, or retreat center, in India. By now, John's drug and alcohol use was out of control. At the ashram, he meditated instead of abusing drugs, cleansing

In March 1968, the Beatles took part in a training session in Transcendental Meditation, or TM. TM is a method of finding a sense of harmony with oneself and the world through chanting and meditation. In this photo, Jane Asher (Paul's girlfriend), Paul, and George are seated in front of guru Maharishi Mahesh Yogi. During the Beatles' stay at the ashram in India, the members of the band had one of the most productive periods in their history.

his body physically and spiritually. George, too, gave up drugs while on retreat.

The other Beatles weren't quite so keen on the ashram. Ringo and his wife Maureen missed their children so much that they left after just two weeks. Paul and his girlfriend Jane managed to stay a bit longer. But, after a month, they too had had enough and headed for home.

During his few weeks in India, though, Paul's creativity flowed. He "wrote like mad," and so did John. In the end, the pair penned more than 40 songs while at the ashram—some together, some individually. It was the most productive time of their lives in terms of songwriting.

That summer, they recorded more than 30 of the new tunes, enough to fill three albums. In the end, they edited the collection down to a two-album set. The release was officially called The Beatles, but it will always be known as "The White Album," because of its completely blank white cover. Released in November 1968 in the UK and the United States, the White

Album was called "disorganized, rough, and unfocused," by some critics. Others said it was "the richest and most diverse single work ever produced by the Beatles." Either way, fans loved it, buying almost two million copies in its first week on store shelves.

For the Beatles, the White Album marked another turning point. It was a collection of songs written, and sometimes even recorded, by *individual* members of the band. For some of the songs, different members of the band recorded their parts in separate studios, often with different producers. In this respect, the album was a sign of the growing distance between the members of the group—personally and creatively—as each Beatle began to develop his own style and approach to music. Even the traditional group portrait was missing from the package, replaced inside the album with four individual portraits of the lads. "For the first time in their careers, the Beatles were presenting themselves as four individuals and not as the collective 'band,' " wrote biographer Bruce Glassman.

At the same time, tensions between band members were on the rise. Jealousy, resentment, disagreements, infighting, and egos were flaring. "The Beatles were getting real tense with each other," said John.

One cause of the friction was John's new love, an artist named Yoko Ono.

Life with Yoko

John met Yoko sometime around 1965 or 1966, under circumstances that had to do either with work she was doing on a book on music or with

The BEATLES

In contrast to the amount of color and information displayed on the Sgt. Pepper's Lonely Hearts Club Band *cover, the cover of the album entitled simply* The Beatles *featured as little information as possible. Popularly known as "The White Album," this record came in a sleeve that featured just the title and a unique serial number, either embossed in raised white letters or printed in gray.*

HEY JULIAN

John's breakup with his wife Cynthia led to one of the Beatles' greatest songs ever. After the separation, Paul went to visit Cynthia and her young son Julian. To help cheer Julian up, Paul made up a song with comforting lyrics for the boy: "Hey Jules—don't make it bad. Take a sad song and make it better." As he sang the tune for Julian, Paul realized it had potential. Eventually, he changed Jules to Jude and wrote what John later called "one of Paul's masterpieces." Released as a single in August 1968, "Hey Jude" sold two million copies in two weeks.

John Lennon and Yoko Ono are shown at the London opening of You Are Here, *an art exhibit that they created together in July 1968.*

an exhibit of her art that she was staging at a London gallery. By 1968, John's involvement with Yoko and her art evolved into work on which they joined forces, and ultimately to an intimate relationship. In the summer of 1968, John and Cynthia split up after six years of marriage.

At the same time, Yoko began to get involved with the band's recording sessions. The Beatles had never permitted anyone in the recording studio with them, especially not wives or girlfriends. But suddenly, during studio sessions for the White Album (*The Beatles*), John started bringing Yoko. Not only did she attend the sessions, she *participated*, infuriating Paul, George, and Ringo. In addition to contributing as a songwriter with John on one of the tracks, Yoko interrupted, criticized, gave orders to technicians, and even joined the group by singing into John's microphone on occasion. Ringo got so fed up with the increasing tensions among the members, and the countless delays and complications during the sessions, that he quit the band in August. This left the other three to fill in for him on drums on several tracks while they pleaded with him to return. Two weeks later, they convinced him to come back.

At the end of November 1968, a week after the White Album was released, John and Yoko riled up the rest of the Beatles even more when they released their own album. In the words of one critic, it was "a collection of mumblings and ambient noise" called *Unfinished Music No. 1: Two Virgins*. To most critics and fans alike, even more unsettling than the noise on the record was the cover, which showed John and Yoko completely naked.

By most standards, the photo was considered indecent, so the album came in a plain brown wrapper. (John would later describe the photo as one of "two slightly overweight ex-junkies.") The fuss over the John and Yoko album threatened to upstage the White Album's release, further angering Paul, George, and Ringo.

Soon after that, John decided his time with the Beatles was over. "The togetherness had gone," he said. "There was no longer any spark." Like Ringo, though, he soon came back to the band, convinced that creating another album would pull the group together again.

Before long, it was George's turn to snap. One day, he became so annoyed with the squabbling and criticism among the musicians, he stormed out of a recording session. He, too, returned after a few days—but it was clear that artistic differences, bickering, and business conflicts had started pulling the band mates in different directions. The Beatles were falling apart.

THE ANTICS OF "JOHNANDYOKO"

When John met Yoko Ono, she was an artist with a flair for the dramatic. In fact, much of her work was performance art, which, as its name suggests, combines visual art with dramatic performance. As John became more involved with Yoko, his life became less and less "usual," even by Beatles standards. In addition to becoming more outspoken and active on issues such as the war in Vietnam, John and Yoko chose ways of expressing themselves that were more dramatic. Together, they staged a number of "bed-ins" for peace. They stayed in bed together—usually in hotel rooms, and usually with many reporters and photographers present—for days or weeks on end. During one of these bed-ins in Montreal, John wrote his famous first solo single "Give Peace a Chance." The song quickly became an anthem for the anti-war movement, and it is still sung at peace rallies today. They once delivered a press conference from inside a giant white bag. After a car accident, an injured Yoko attended Beatles' recording sessions—in a rented hospital bed.

In 1969, John officially changed his name to John Winston Ono Lennon and began signing his name as "johnandyoko." The couple's drug use was extensive for several years. Following their withdrawal from heroin addictions, John wrote a song called "Cold Turkey."

John and Yoko on the first day of their Bed-in for Peace at the Amsterdam Hilton Hotel in the Netherlands, 1969.

The Beatles Are History

Despite the personal conflicts, John, Paul, George, and Ringo agreed to create another project together. The plan was to record an album and document the recording sessions to make another film at the same time. The music would be simpler than the music they had created in recent recording sessions—more in line with early Beatles sounds.

In January 1969, the young men headed into the recording studio to get started on the album they were going to call Get Back. It was clear from the beginning it wasn't going to work. Paul was bossy. George and Ringo stormed out. John showed up high on drugs and, as always, with Yoko by his side interfering with recording sessions.

By the end of the month, the foursome could barely stand working together. Still, the film crew needed a live performance to wrap up the

WE ALL LIVE IN A YELLOW SUBMARINE...

In the summer of 1968, a group of animators developed a feature-length movie with cartoon versions of the Beatles as the main characters. Named *Yellow Submarine,* it was very loosely based on the Beatles' 1966 song of the same name. The movie was a huge hit among moviegoers and critics alike.

A live-action appearance by the Beatles lasts about a minute at the end of the film. Other than that brief appearance, and a number of hit songs and previously unreleased tunes, the entire movie was produced without the participation of the Beatles themselves. Actors provided the voices of the characters, and the Beatles were said to be unenthusiastic about the entire idea of a full-length animated Beatles movie.

This all took place in the middle of the tumultuous time when the Beatles were in a state of nearly constant conflict. That, plus the fact that this would be one easy way to fulfill their three-movie contract with United Artists studios, probably convinced them to give the project their blessing. After the lads had gone their separate ways, they admitted that they actually liked the finished product, which to this day is considered a classic of animated cinema.

documentary. Ringo mentioned that the Apple building, where they were recording, had a rooftop garden. It would be perfect!

On January 30, 1969, the band, film crew, and technicians secretly set up for a performance on the roof. Just before noon, the Beatles started playing a concert that could be heard throughout the West End of London. Word spread, and crowds started to gather on the street below—after all, the Beatles hadn't performed together publicly in almost three years! Once the traffic ground to a halt, police showed up to shut the show down. But for a short 42 minutes, the old magic of the Fab Four had returned. "We turned back into those brothers and musicians," said Ringo.

Filming for the documentary wrapped up the next day, and the lads went back to the studio to finish up their recording sessions. Even though the rooftop performance had been brilliant, the studio work wasn't. Nobody could figure out how to pull it all together into an album. So while the filmmakers' work on the documentary continued, the Beatles gave up on the album project for the time being.

In March, Paul married photographer Linda Eastman. A week later, John married Yoko. Neither Beatle invited his former best friend to his wedding. By then, John and Paul's dislike for each other had become very public, and rumors of a Beatle breakup were spreading again. The bickering among all four Beatles was obvious. Through the spring and summer in 1969, the four lads went their separate ways. John and Yoko worked on a film project. Paul helped other musicians with private projects.

"I think by 1968, we were all a bit exhausted spiritually. I think generally there was a feel of, 'Yeah, it's great to be famous, it's great to be rich, but what's it all for?'"

Paul
McCartney

Ringo acted in a movie, and George recorded a solo album.

Meanwhile, the Beatles' company Apple was also falling apart. It needed new management, but the foursome couldn't even agree on whom they wanted to hire. Eventually three of the four—all but Paul—agreed on record company executive Allen Klein. Immediately, Klein fired most of the Apple staff and closed all branches of the business except Apple Records.

At Last: *Abbey Road*

Somehow, the Beatles managed to pull themselves back together in the recording studio in the summer of 1969. Somehow, through all the clashing and chaos, they managed to pull together their final recorded album *Abbey Road*. (Their final released album *Let It Be* had been recorded, but would not be released until 1970.) On the spur of the moment, they decided to shoot the album cover on the street outside the studio.

"'I'd like to say 'thank you' on behalf of the group and ourselves, and I hope we passed the audition.'"

John on the album version of "Get Back," in response to scattered applause during the Beatles' rooftop concert in 1969

THE WOMEN WITH THE BEATLES

When John Lennon wed his longtime girlfriend Cynthia Powell in 1962, he became the first Beatle to get married. The two had met in art school, and Cynthia was pregnant when they got married. After John met Yoko Ono, he and Cynthia drifted apart. One day, Cynthia came home after being out of the country and found John and Yoko together. Cynthia and John divorced in 1968, and John and Yoko married in March 1969.

Paul McCartney was engaged to his girlfriend of five years Jane Asher, when he met photographer Linda Eastman. Paul married Linda in 1969. Sadly, "lovely Linda," as Paul called her, died from cancer in 1998. Four years later, he married former model Heather Mills. They divorced in 2006. In 2011, Paul married New York businesswoman Nancy Shevell.

George Harrison's first marriage—to model/actress Pattie Boyd—also ended in divorce, when Pattie left George for his friend and fellow musician Eric Clapton. In 1978, George married Olivia Arias, an assistant at a record company, and the two were together for the rest of George's life.

Ringo Starr wed Maureen Cox in 1965. They had three children together before divorcing 10 years later. In 1980, he met actress Barbara Bach on the set of the movie *Caveman*. They married a year later and are still together.

Shown at the April 1981 wedding of Ringo Starr and actress Barbara Bach (both in the center) are (left) George and Olivia Harrison and (right) Paul and Linda McCartney. Linda is holding her and Paul's son James, and Barbara's son Gianni is shown in the front.

The shot of the four of them walking across a crosswalk has become one of the Beatles' most famous photographs.

Toward the end of the *Abbey Road* studio sessions, John announced he was "divorcing" the band. Unlike other times when one or another of the Beatles had quit, they all knew that this time, John meant it. Record producer George Martin convinced the foursome to keep the news quiet so as not to disrupt sensitive business deals or the September release of *Abbey Road*.

Some critics have called *Abbey Road* one of the greatest albums of all time. From then on, though, the four Beatles quietly went their separate ways, working on individual projects. On April 10, 1970, Paul went public with the band's breakup. He announced his resignation from the group, officially ending the extraordinary alliance that had been the Beatles.

This British postage stamp honors Abbey Road, *the Beatles' final recorded album. Like other Beatles albums,* Abbey Road *has one of the most recognized record covers in the world.*

FOR THE RECORD... PAUL IS NOT DEAD

In the fall of 1969, a student newspaper in Iowa printed an article saying Paul McCartney was dead and had been replaced by a look-alike performer. A month later, radio stations in Detroit and New York picked up the story, which soon spread across America. The rumor was that Paul had been killed in a car accident three years earlier. The reports were supposedly proven to be true by clues the remaining Beatles left in their music—when it was played backwards—and in photos and album cover art. The story was, of course, not true. Today, having celebrated his 70th birthday in June 2012, Paul McCartney is still alive and well, but the "Paul is dead" rumor still pops up every once in a while.

Chapter 6
The Beatles Go Solo

In April 1970, a week after news of the Fab Four's breakup went public, Paul released his first solo album, with a clearly solo title: *McCartney*. A month later, the Beatles' final album—the one they had recorded and put aside in 1969—was released. Five days after that, the documentary about the making of that final album—featuring the footage of the now-famous rooftop concert—made its world premiere. *Get Back*, the original title of the album-and-film project, was changed to *Let It Be*. With that, a magical era in music history was over, and the age of solo careers had begun.

John Lennon: Father, Writer, Activist

In December 1970, John Lennon released his first solo album. A year later, his second album *Imagine* was released. The title track *Imagine* became Lennon's signature song.

With its 1970 release, Let It Be, *shown on this stamp, became the last "official" Beatles album. Paul McCartney was not happy with some of the enhanced production techniques of the album. In 2003, he remixed and remastered (performed an audio upgrade) most of the songs, removing the elaborate orchestration and studio chatter. The name of the stripped-down version was* Let It Be... Naked.

In 2004, *Rolling Stone* magazine named "Imagine" as the third-best song of all time (after songs by Bob Dylan and the Rolling Stones). As John continued his post-Beatles musical career, he often collaborated with his wife Yoko Ono. The couple moved to New York City in 1971. Aside from being a musician, John was a noted writer, artist, and anti-war activist.

In 1972, he and Yoko performed a pair of benefit concerts at Madison Square Garden for a school in New York for people with intellectual disabilities. Those concerts were to be John's last full-length performances.

Around this same time, John's words and actions against the Vietnam War led to efforts by the U.S. government to have him deported from the United States. Starting in 1972, he spent many months engaged in legal battles to be given permission to live in the United States. Yoko, who was already a permanent U.S. resident, became part of John's struggle. Others in the nation also took up their cause and, in 1976, he was granted the status of permanent resident in the United States.

During these years between the early and mid-1970s, John collaborated with such famous musicians as Elton John, David Bowie, and Frank Zappa. He released a series of successful albums until 1975, when he disappeared from the music scene altogether. That year, on John's 35th birthday Yoko gave birth to the couple's son Sean. John became a stay-at-home dad for the next five years, until he realized he missed having music in his life.

People wore buttons like this to show their support for John's struggle against U.S. government efforts to have him deported in the early 1970s.

In 1980, John and Yoko wrote, recorded, and released *Double Fantasy,* which topped *Imagine* as John's best-selling non-Beatles album ever. Three weeks after the album came out, just as John was getting back into the public eye, the world was forced to say goodbye to the peace-loving and often troubled musician. On December 8, 1980, a crazed fan named Mark David Chapman shot and killed John Lennon outside the Dakota—the New York apartment building where he and Yoko lived.

CRIME AND PUNISHMENT

In the late afternoon of December 8, 1980, John Lennon and Yoko Ono stepped out of their New York City apartment building. Their *Double Fantasy* album had just been released, so there were always a few fans on the sidewalk hoping for the ex-Beatle's autograph. That day, John signed a *Double Fantasy* album cover for a 25-year-old former security guard named Mark David Chapman.

Seven hours later, when John and Yoko returned home after a recording session, the same young man was waiting for them. He called out, "Mr. Lennon!" Then he shot John five times, killing him almost instantly. Chapman had been obsessed with John, convinced the rock star was "a phony" who deserved to die. He later pleaded guilty to second-degree murder. He has been in prison in New York state ever since. Chapman has applied for—and been denied—parole seven times, most recently in August 2012.

"When John Lennon was killed in December 1980, the world was in complete mourning. Here was a man who only called for peace and love, and he was gunned down outside of his apartment in New York City."

David Eisenbach, cultural historian

Displaying a popular photo of John wearing a "New York City" shirt, fans gather in Ottawa, Ontario, to sing "Give Peace a Chance." The date is December 8, 2010—the 30th anniversary of John's murder in New York on the same date in 1980.

Paul McCartney: Music Legend, Knight, and Superstar Senior

A year after he left the Beatles, Paul McCartney, along with wife Linda (a singer and keyboard player), formed a new band called Wings. For 10 years, the band enjoyed great success. They toured the world and produced 10 albums and numerous hit singles, including "Band on the Run," "Baby I'm Amazed," "Live and Let Die," and "Jet."

After John was killed, Paul refused to risk going on tour, a decision that led to the end of Wings in 1981. Still, Paul continued to write, play, and record new music, collaborating with Michael Jackson, Stevie Wonder, Ringo Starr, Elvis Costello, and the Royal Liverpool Philharmonic, among other artists. He started touring again in 1989 and hasn't stopped since.

In 1997, Paul became Sir Paul when Queen Elizabeth II knighted him for his contributions to music. He was inducted into the Rock and Roll Hall of Fame in 1999, and he organized the post-9/11 Concert for New York in 2001.

In 2012, at age 70, Paul played an outdoor concert in London's Hyde Park with American rocker Bruce Springsteen. He played at the Diamond Jubilee Concert to celebrate Queen Elizabeth's 60 years on the throne, and he performed at the opening ceremonies for the London 2012 Olympic Games.

With a career that has—so far—spanned more than 50 years, Sir Paul's concerts continue to sell out around the world. He holds the record as the most successful musician and songwriter in pop music history, and he shows no signs of slowing down. "Why would I retire?" he said recently. "Sit at home and watch TV? No thanks. I'd rather be out playing."

George Harrison: Humanitarian, Filmmaker, and Homebody

The year the Beatles broke up, George Harrison released a three-record album, *All Things Must Pass*, his first and most successful solo album. His song "My Sweet Lord" became a #1 single, but it also became the subject of a lawsuit because of its similarity to the Chiffons' 1963 song "He's So Fine." Harrison lost the lawsuit and had to pay almost $600,000 in damages. Nonetheless, both the album and the song have been acclaimed for their content and musical quality. Despite the success of such Harrison-written Beatles hits as "While My Guitar Gently Weeps," "Here Comes the Sun," and "Something," George's songwriting career was understandably overshadowed by the incredible success of the Lennon-McCartney dynamo. Many were therefore pleasantly

Joined by George Harrison's widow Olivia, actor Tom Hanks, and George's son Dhani, Paul playfully points out the Hollywood Walk of Fame star that was placed in honor of George in 2009.

In this photograph, taken in 1996, George Harrison is shown chanting in India. Since a visit to India in 1966, George became an admirer of Indian music, culture, and religion. From the mid-1960s on, Hinduism became an important part of his personal life and his music. Throughout his life, until his death in 2001, he spoke often of his mystical beliefs and the healing power of chanting and meditation.

surprised that the "quiet Beatle" had, within a year of the Beatles' breakup, put together such a large and powerful collection of songs.

In 1973, with Indian musician Ravi Shankar and the help of Ringo Starr, Bob Dylan, and other prominent musicians from the 1960s and 1970s, George staged the Concert for Bangladesh in New York City. His goal was to raise awareness about, and money for, refugees from this war-torn region of South Asia. The similarly titled three-record album, which was produced to aid the relief effort, was also a huge success.

Over the years, George continued to produce albums and work with celebrated musicians, including Bob Dylan, Tom Petty, Roy Orbison, and Jeff Lynne of the Electric Light Orchestra, with whom he formed a super-group, the Traveling Wilburys. The members of the group shared singing and songwriting duties, and each of them brought a distinctive style to a sound that was new and successful. This was particularly surprising considering the high-profile nature of its members. He also started his own record label and a film production company that made 27 movies before George sold his share in the business.

In the 1980s, George became a bit of a homebody, keeping busy with two new hobbies—gardening and collecting cars. After a 1998 bout of throat cancer and a near-fatal multiple stabbing by a deranged fan in 1999 (during which his wife Olivia saved his life by beating the attacker with a fire iron), George died of lung and brain cancer in 2001 at age 58.

Ringo Starr: Concert Master, Actor, Animal Lover

Since the Beatles' official breakup, Ringo Starr has released 16 solo studio albums, 10 live albums, and 24 singles. In 1971, "It Don't Come Easy" became a signature hit for Ringo, and his most successful album was 1973's *Ringo*. It featured performances and songs by a variety of musical talents, most notably all four former Beatles in various combinations. "Photograph," "Oh My My," and "You're Sixteen" were big sellers from that album.

Ringo has also appeared in TV commercials, narrated a children's TV series, and had a guest-starring role—playing himself—on the animated TV series *The Simpsons*. He has acted in films, been nominated for a Daytime Emmy Award, and has a star on the Hollywood Walk of Fame. In 1981, six years after he and Maureen divorced, he married actress Barbara Bach, whom he had met on the set of the movie *Caveman*.

In 1989, Ringo put together a band of all-star musicians for a three-month tour through the United States. Since then, he has toured through North America and Europe with 13 different versions of Ringo Starr & His All-Starr Band.

Ringo, now in his 70s, has supported many causes during his career. Today, he is raising awareness of the near-extinction of certain species of rhinoceros, with his website plea to "Save the Rhino."

Ringo is shown playing with his All-Starr Band in Paris in 2011.

Ringo at a press conference while touring in Ukraine in 2011.

BEATLE BABIES

John Lennon had his son Julian with his first wife Cynthia Powell, and son Sean with his second wife Yoko Ono. Both sons are musicians. Julian, who is also a photographer, has released seven albums. Sean is a singer, songwriter, bass player, music producer, and actor.

Paul McCartney had three children with his first wife Linda. Their best-known child is famous fashion designer Stella McCartney. Eldest daughter Mary followed in her mother's footsteps and became a photographer, while son James is a musician who has worked with his father on many projects. Paul also has a 10-year-old daughter named Beatrice, from his second marriage to Heather Mills.

George Harrison and his wife Olivia had one son Dhani, who is also a musician. Ringo Starr had three children with his first wife Maureen. His eldest son Zak Starkey is a successful rock drummer and has worked with The Who, Oasis, Iron Maiden and, of course, Ringo Starr & His All-Starr Band. Zak's brother Jason is also a drummer like his dad. Their sister Lee Starkey is a make-up artist and fashion designer.

James McCartney

Stella McCartney

Dhani Harrison

Sean Lennon

Julian Lennon

Zak Starkey

Magical Brotherhood, Musical Pioneers, Unbroken Success Story

The Beatles split up more than 40 years ago, but they remain the bestselling band in history. Forty-five new Beatles albums—greatest hits, live albums, and never-before-heard song collections—have been released in North America and Europe since 1970. The Beatles earned seven Grammy Awards, an Academy Award for best original film score for *Let It Be*, and 15 awards from the British Academy of Songwriters, Composers and Authors. In 1988, they were inducted into the Rock and Roll Hall of Fame—the first year they were eligible for this honor. In 2008, *Billboard* magazine named the Beatles #1 on its Hot 100 Artists list.

All four Beatles continued to collaborate with each other, here and there, during their solo careers. After John died, the surviving Beatles created a project called *The Beatles Anthology*, a history of the Beatles told through a documentary television series, a three-part double-album record set, and a book. About 400 million people watched the 1995 TV series, and Volume 1 of the album set sold more than 850,000 copies in its first week on the market.

Clearly, music lovers still crave the Beatles—including young people who weren't even alive when the four lads from Liverpool were together. Melissa Joyce is one such fan. She was eight years old when she first heard a Beatles song. Today, in her 20s, she can still appreciate the joy that came from that first encounter:

"For me, the Beatles represent happiness, love, peace, and laughter. There is magic in their music that makes me feel absolutely happy, and makes me smile. I might not have been born at the time or been a teen in the '60s, but I feel like I am when listening to them."

In their heyday, the Beatles changed the way we listened to music, creating albums filled with innovative sounds and technologies that continue to influence musicians of today. The Beatles created the first music videos and turned the rock concert into a cultural event. They transformed the simple record album from a collection of songs into a form of storytelling through music. They influenced the fashion of the day and led a global cultural revolution. The Beatles were trendsetters who also happened to have talent. "The Beatles represent one of the few times in musical history when the most popular was also the best," wrote biographer Chris Ingham.

Certainly, some of the Beatles' ongoing appeal must be credited to smart marketing and technological advance. In addition to regular album releases are re-releases using

"The Fab Four created their own, unique and original world of The Beatles. In this world, there were wonderful things, people lived in 'nowhere,' yellow submarines were abundant, guitars were crying, an octopus invited you to its garden, Lucy soared into the heavens, and so on. This magical space was open to anyone who wanted to visit."

Cultural commentator Anton Evseyev

new technology. In 2009, after a four-year remastering project, the Beatles' entire catalog of music was re-released on CD. In 2010, all the studio albums, and a number of compilation albums, were made available on iTunes. Their films have also been remastered and re-released.

Today there is a *Beatles: Rock Band* video game and a Beatles-inspired Cirque du Soleil show called *Love*. Beatles tribute bands tour the world year after year; hundreds of authors have written hundreds of books about the Beatles; and thousands of musicians have covered, or recorded, nearly every Beatles song ever written.

Historians, journalists, and scholars have studied the Beatles from every possible angle, trying to unlock the secret to their never-ending appeal. Was it simply their music and lyrics? Were they just in the right place at the right time? Was it their quirky personalities? Maybe it was the mop top hair. "We've all heard the what, the who, and the how of their story," said one researcher. "What we still don't know is the why."

For fans, it probably doesn't matter why the Beatles skyrocketed to fame, or why they are still capturing hearts half a century later. They just did— and they will likely continue to cast their magical mystery spell for generations to come.

Chronology

1940 Ringo Starr born as Richard Starkey July 7; John Lennon born Oct. 9.

1942 Paul McCartney born June 18.

1943 George Harrison born Feb. 25.

1956 John forms skiffle band called the Quarrymen; Paul plays first-ever solo performance at a summer resort; Paul's mother dies of cancer.

1957 Paul plays with Quarrymen.

1958 George joins Quarrymen; John's mother dies.

1959 Quarrymen play opening night concert at Casbah Coffee Club; Ringo joins Rory Storm and the Hurricanes.

1960 John's friend Stu Sutcliffe joins band on bass guitar; group changes name to the Silver Beetles; drummer Pete Best joins band, now called the Beatles; group begins playing clubs in Hamburg, Germany.

1961 Play at Liverpool's Cavern Club; return to Hamburg; Stu quits band; Paul changes to bass; record two songs with singer Tony Sheridan; Brian Epstein becomes Beatles' manager.

1962 Return to Hamburg; learn Stu died day before they arrived; get record deal at EMI Records; Pete fired; Ringo joins Beatles; John marries Cynthia Powell; release their first single, "Love Me Do," which reaches #17 on charts.

1963 Second single, "Please Please Me," released, goes to #1; record first album, also titled *Please Please Me;* British press coins term "Beatlemania"; 10,000 screaming fans greet Beatles at London's Heathrow Airport upon return from Sweden; perform for Royal Family.

1964 Arrive in U.S. for *The Ed Sullivan Show* and live concerts; thousands of screaming fans greet them at JFK airport; 73 million watch debut on Sullivan; make first movie *A Hard Day's Night;* records hold top five spots on charts in U.S.; tour Australia and New Zealand, where they are mobbed by fans.

1965 Make second movie *Help!;* inducted as Member of the Order of the British Empire; meet idol Elvis Presley; perform at Shea Stadium for record crowd of 56,000.

1966 In interview, John says Beatles are "more popular than Jesus," prompting boycotts of music, burning of albums, and death threats; perform in San Francisco for their last-ever concert.

1967 Release what many consider their greatest album *Sgt. Pepper's Lonely Hearts Club Band;* Brian Epstein dies of a drug overdose.

1968 Create Apple Corps, consisting of Apple Records and other businesses; visit India to meditate and study Eastern philosophy; while there, John and Paul write more than 40 new songs; John and Cynthia divorce; one of Beatles' greatest songs, "Hey Jude," released as single, selling two million copies in first two weeks; John starts bringing Yoko Ono to recording studio, against wishes of band mates; personal conflicts among the four Beatles—especially John and Paul—lead three of the four (all but Paul) to quit the band; each returns, but Beatles are beginning to fall apart.

1969 Start recording an album and filming a documentary; project will be released a year later as *Let It Be;* band plays rooftop concert, briefly reviving the magic; Paul marries photographer Linda Eastman; John marries Yoko; Beatles record final studio album *Abbey Road;* All Apple Corps branches close except Apple Records; John announces he is "divorcing" the Beatles.

1970 Paul goes public with announcement of band's break-up, releases first solo album; John and George also release solo albums.

1971 John releases *Imagine* album and single; he and Yoko move to New York City; Paul and Linda form new band called Wings.

1980 Mark David Chapman murders John Lennon.

1988 Beatles inducted into Rock and Roll Hall of Fame.

1989 Ringo creates All-Starr Band, which regularly changes musicians and is still doing tours.

1995 Paul, George, and Ringo pull together documentary film/album/ book project called *The Beatles Anthology.*

1997 Paul knighted, becomes Sir Paul.

2001 George dies of cancer.

2002 Paul and Ringo join 25 other musicians to perform at Concert for George, a memorial and fundraiser in honor of George Harrison.

2012 Paul plays at Queen Elizabeth's Diamond Jubilee Concert and at the London 2012 Olympic Games.

Glossary

activist A person who believes in a cause, issue or political system, and takes action to promote that belief

alliance A group of people who have a close relationship and shared goal

ambient noise Background sound

appendicitis A dangerous and painful inflammation and swelling of the appendix, which is a small tube in the intestines

ashram A retreat center for spiritual study

collaborated Worked together on a project

common-law partner A member of a couple who lives together but is not married

compilation album A collection of previously recorded songs

cultural revolution A time of great change in society, in terms of civil rights, belief systems, politics, and music, literature, and art

embody To give form to an idea or concept

epiphany A moment of sudden insight or understanding

guru A person who is viewed as an expert, leader, or teacher in a certain field

heyday A period of time when somebody is at one's prime, or peak, in terms of success, popularity, or power

humanitarian A person devoted to helping others, relieving the suffering of others, and improving the lives of others

induct To include someone in a highly respected organization

jamming Playing music with other musicians in an informal setting, not a concert

knight A man who was not born into royalty, but has been given a royal title by a king or queen and is entitled to have "Sir" before his name

lyrics Words of a song

memorabilia Collectors' items, or objects that once belonged to a famous person or are otherwise connected with a famous person or event

merchant sailor A crew member on a ship used for transporting cargo or people; usually not involved in military activities, but may be called upon during wartime

midwife A health-care professional who supports pregnant women and helps deliver their babies

parole Early release from prison with conditions and rules attached

philosophical Thinking about big issues and deeper meanings in life and life events

pleurisy A serious lung disease that involves an inflammation of the lining of the lungs and impairs breathing

pop culture Short for "popular culture," a collection of ideas, trends, fashion, music, art, movies, and other elements that are in style at a given point in time

principality A state ruled by royalty

promotional items Merchandise or souvenirs sold to promote an event, a band, or other artist or event

psychedelic Relating to drugs, particularly those that create hallucinations and other altered states of consciousness; to music associated with drug themes and musical experimentation; and to intense, often swirling colors

remaster To use updated technology to remake an audio or video project

riff A musical phrase, or group of notes within a longer musical passage

set A series of songs played in a concert, or in one segment of a concert (as in song set)

signature song A distinctive song that is identified with a particular musician

single An individual song, released on its own, not as part of an album of songs (as in a record single)

spirituals Religious songs that were created by slaves in the American South and were derived from a combination of European hymns and African musical elements

stilted Stiff, awkward, uncomfortable

stoned Under the influence of a mind-altering substance; same as "high"

sullen Bad-tempered and quiet

track A layer of sound or audio recording that can be blended with other tracks, or layers of sound (as in four-track recording)

tribute band A band that copies and imitates a very famous band

tutor A teacher who works with a student one-on-one, rather than in a classroom

upstage To take the focus away from someone else and put it onto oneself

Further Information

Books

Edgers, Geoff. *Who Were the Beatles?* New York, NY: Grosset and Dunlap, 2006.

Spitz, Bob. *Yeah! Yeah! Yeah! The Beatles, Beatlemania, and the Music That Changed the World.* New York, NY: Little, Brown and Company, 2007.

The Beatles. *The Beatles Anthology.* San Francisco, CA: Chronicle Books, 2000.

Videos

The Beatles Anthology (DVD). EMI Video, 2003.

A Hard Day's Night (DVD). Miramax, 2002.

Yellow Submarine (DVD). Apple Corps, 2012.

Online

WEBSITES:
www.beatles.com
The official Beatles website. It lists every album, its history, and every song with lyrics. It features photos, videos, news articles, and a short history of the Beatles.

www.beatlesagain.com
Called *The Internet Beatles Album,* this site offers an excellent collection of articles, photos, and sound and video clips about the Beatles.

www.beatlesbible.com/
The Beatles Bible: Not Quite as Popular as Jesus… is probably the most thorough Beatles website out there. It features biographies, discographies, a Beatles map that shows locations of significant events in the Fab Four's career, Beatles online stores, special features, song lyrics, and a fan forum.

www.beatles-history.net/

Titled *The Complete Online History of the Beatles,* this website provides another good documentation of the Beatles, their history, and discography. It has lots of photos, videos, and links to other articles.

www.beatlesnews.com

All the latest news about the Beatles. It is updated daily and lists articles about the Fab Four, their families, and anything written about them. It also has a "Today in Beatles History" section and links to other interesting websites.

www.mersey-beat.com

Mersey Beat was a twice-a-month newspaper produced in Liverpool from 1960 to 1964, founded by one of John Lennon's art school friends. The publication carried news about bands and clubs in Liverpool. The website contains an archive of articles from *Mersey Beat*, with a full section of Beatles articles.

AUDIO AND VIDEO CLIPS (also check links to other clips on these sites):
www.youtube.com/watch?v=hSdgFc5g4f0

Audio recording of the Quarrymen performing the day they met Paul McCartney.

www.youtube.com/watch?v=AR39ZyV76a4

The Beatles play the Cavern Club in 1962. This video was recorded for a TV show. At the very end, you can hear a fan yell, "We want Pete," meaning Pete Best, the drummer who had just been replaced by Ringo Starr.

www.beatlesbible.com/1963/11/04/live-royal-command-performance/

The Beatles play at the Royal Command Performance for the Queen Mother, 1963.

www.youtube.com/watch?v=WHuRusAlw-Y

The Beatles' first appearance on *The Ed Sullivan Show,* on February 1964.

www.thebeatles.com/#/video/The_Beatles_At_Shea_Stadium2

Amazing full-color footage showing security measures and effect of the screaming fans as the Fab Four arrive for their concert at New York's Shea Stadium in 1965.

Index

About the Author

Diane Dakers was born and raised in Toronto and now makes her home in Victoria, British Columbia. A specialist in arts and cultural issues, Diane has been a newspaper, magazine, TV, and radio journalist since 1991. The only one of the Beatles she has ever seen in concert is Ringo Starr, on his first tour with his All-Starr Band in 1989. Diane has also had the pleasure of riding through the streets of Victoria, BC, in John Lennon's psychedelic Rolls Royce, enjoying the smiles of everyone who saw the madcap car.